BODIES IN THE BACK GARDEN

BODIES IN THE BACK GARDEN

TRUE STORIES OF BRUTAL MURDERS CLOSE TO HOME

NIGEL CAWTHORNE

JOHN BLAKE

Published by John Blake Publishing Ltd,
3 Bramber Court, 2 Bramber Road,
London W14 9PB, England

www.johnblakepublishing.co.uk

www.facebook.com/Johnblakepub ⓕ
twitter.com/johnblakepub ⓣ

First published in paperback in 2014

ISBN: 978-1-78219-986-1

British Library Cataloguing-in-Publication Data:

A catalogue record for this book is available from the British Library.

Design by www.envydesign.co.uk

Printed in Great Britain by CPI Group (UK) Ltd

5 7 9 10 8 6 4

Papers used by John Blake Publishing are natural, recyclable products made from
wood grown in sustainable forests. The manufacturing processes conform to the
environmental regulations of the country of origin.

Every attempt has been made to contact the relevant copyright-holders,
but some were unobtainable. We would be grateful if the appropriate
people could contact us.

CONTENTS

INTRODUCTION

On 9 October 2013, two bodies were found in the back garden of a semi-detached house at 2 Blenheim Close, Forest Town, on the outskirts of Mansfield in Nottinghamshire. Post-mortem examinations of the remains revealed that each victim had died after a single shot to the head. The couple were identified as husband and wife William and Patricia Wycherley, who had disappeared from the property some 15 years earlier. Neighbours thought they had gone abroad.

On the evening of 30 October, the Wycherley's daughter and son-in-law – Susan Edwards, 55, and Christopher John Edwards, 57 – were arrested at St Pancras International railway station in London. Four days later, they were charged with the murders of the Wycherleys between 1 and 31 May 1998. The couple had lived in a cul-de-sac just 150 yards from Susan's parents' home, which was at the end of the terrace. While they told the police they had 'no fixed abode', it was thought that Christopher Edwards was still living there, while Susan Edwards had been living abroad before her arrest.

Mr Wycherley would have been 100 years old, and his wife 79, had they still been alive. Mr Wycherley had been a wartime veteran merchant seaman; they had lived in the two-bedroom house for 11 years before their disappearance. The house was sold in 2005 and the new residents had no inkling that the previous occupants' bodies were hidden on the premises. The Wycherleys' relatives continued to get birthday and Christmas cards, which appeared to have been signed by the couple until around 2009. Neither was ever reported missing.

Detective Chief Inspector Rob Griffin, who led the investigation, said, 'Bones were discovered in a grave in the garden. People we have spoken to, to date, have described the Wycherleys as reclusive. They kept themselves to themselves and it didn't appear they had many regular friends or associates.'

One resident of Blenheim Crescent said, when she had been told that the Wycherleys had emigrated, 'I found it a bit weird that they would have done that, because that's something you do in your fifties and they seemed to be quite elderly. We have been in the garden having barbecues without knowing a few houses away there were two bodies.'

In court, Susan and Christopher Edwards admitted burying her elderly parents in the back garden and theft from a bank account, but denied murdering them.

INTRODUCTION

A month after the bodies of the Wycherleys had been found, the body of a white man was found by workmen in a well in the back garden of a cottage at 11A Audley Drive in the village of Warlingham, Surrey. The well was 2ft in diameter and 11ft deep, with 4ft of water at the bottom. The gruesome job of recovering the remains was left to specialists, including police divers, and it took several hours; the corpse was in a bad state of decay. It had been in the well for around two years, although the body still showed signs of injuries consistent with an assault, prior to being disposed of in the back garden. While the cause of death could not be determined, it was clear that it had been placed there, having been bound before being dropped down the well.

The remains were eventually identified as that of Damian Chlywka, a Polish national who came to live in the UK in 2008. The cottage in Audley Drive was one of several addresses where Chlywka had lived in the area, and he would have been 32 at the time of his discovery.

The police initially arrested seven men, aged between 21-27. After they were interviewed, they were released on police bail. The men arrested were all Polish car-wash workers who lived at the house. One of the men said, 'I want to clear my name. There has been a big mistake. We don't know nothing. We just live there.' Then, on 29 November, two men aged 33 and 41 were arrested. They, too, were bailed.

The body in the well had been found by 17-year-old Jack Duncan and his friend, 21-year-old Rory Mulholland. They were clearing out roses and brambles in the back garden when they found a slab capping the well. 'At first I thought the well was at ground level ... I thought it was ornamental. I didn't think there was a drop in it,' said Mulholland. 'When we pulled up the slab we realised that there was a big drop and we saw a blue tarpaulin at the bottom of the well. At first we thought it was rubbish dumped, so we had a good look around and started moving it, and we slowly came to realise that it was in the shape of a body. You could see the shape of someone's legs and a bottom. Then we flipped the tarp over again and I saw someone's upper thigh. It was definitely a man. I've never smelt anything like it.'

Duncan said that he had trouble sleeping after the discovery. 'It's been really hard to get back to sleep the last couple of nights knowing that you found a dead body,' he said. 'It's just been there ... you don't know how long it's been there. I'm never going to look down a well again.'

A local resident said, 'It is really shocking. You do not expect it here. It is really quite a well-to-do area.'

No one expects bodies buried in the back garden – it seems to be right out of Agatha Christie, though as far as I can recall there is no Christie murder mystery in which the corpse has been interred under the lawn, in a flowerbed or down a garden well; it's much more likely to be found in the library. However, it is easy to believe that the back gardens of St Mary Mead, the village where Miss Marple lived, would be positively groaning with corpses if the residents hadn't considered gardening to be a far more serious a matter than that of mere homicide.

Nevertheless, bodies in the back garden does seem to be a quintessentially English occurrence, even though the body found in the well in Warlingham was that of a Pole. Perhaps it is because the back garden itself seems so quintessentially English. The Scots have rolling moors of heather, the Welsh have hills with sheep grazing on them and the Irish have bogs. Abroad, people live in fancy apartments with backyards – which are not quite the same. But foreigners do murder family, friends and foes, and bury them in that little patch of heaven outside the back door when they can. Certainly Americans, the French, Belgians, Australians and even the Mexicans have tried to get away with it.

The cases in this book obviously deal with those who have not escaped justice – their evil deeds have been discovered and their handiwork disinterred – hopefully to be buried later in a more appropriately respectful location.

In several cases, though, the buried corpse was not discovered for some time, which leads one to suspect that some killers have been successful in secreting the remains of their victims under the vegetable patch. Surely this is another disincentive to eat your greens.

As well as the victims and their loved ones, one has to feel sorry for the next resident of the property. Having spent years shelling out on the mortgage, they are suddenly inundated with an army of policemen in forensic suits erecting a tent on the patio. After they have turned the back garden into a convincing reconstruction of the Battle of Passchendaele, the owners realise that the home they thought was their castle has now become the scene of a gruesome murder and, consequently, unsaleable – except to the mentally unstable. So it has to be pulled down.

Better that, though, than living with bodies in the back garden and wondering, each year, why those blood-red roses you planted by the woodshed are doing so well.

There are other ways to get rid of bodies. Myra Hindley and Ian Brady became notorious as the 'Moors Murderers' because they buried their victims on the bleak exposure of Saddleworth Moor; in Canada, Robert Pickton fed the bodies of numerous prostitutes he murdered to his pigs. Some gangsters feed rivals to the fish, while others favour encasing the corpse in concrete as part of some new motorway construction.

The appeal of burying a body in the back garden – particularly to the English, who have one readily available – is the sheer convenience. In our private plot, shielded from the gaze of nosy neighbours by the leylandii, it is possible to dig a reasonably large hole while pretending to be involved merely in some innocent horticulture or, perhaps, the building of a pond. Then, in the dark of night, one can manhandle the corpse, that has previously been leaking on the carpet, out of the back door and roll it into the pit. A little more shovelling and a trip to the garden centre, and your crime can be skilfully concealed.

Of course, serious criminals can dissolve the body in a vat of acid, or mince up the corpse and distribute it over a local rubbish dump. But for the middle-class criminal who has had little schooling in violent crime, burial in the back garden is the obvious answer.

Now, I am not recommending this course of action. Murder is a heinous crime for which there is no justification whatever the circumstances. Usually, the motives are vile – uncontrollable greed or lust, overweening pride or envy, wrath or simple depravity. However, we are all susceptible to murderous feelings. That is why people who would never think about committing a crime enjoy reading about it.

Having a back garden and a spade to hand, along with a kitchen knife, makes murder domestic. It tames it and brings it within the bounds of possibilities. One could at least imagine killing that unfaithful lover, or the maiden aunt who stands in the way of your inheritance and is about to squander it on some gigolo, and bury them under the petunias.

Up to this point in my life, I have never had a compelling reason to kill anyone, and I certainly would not want to do such a thing frivolously. Besides, I live in central London. It is crowded and, one would think, there would not be very much chance of getting away with it.

But, curiously, I do have a little garden. Not that those living in the comforts of the suburbs would consider it such. At the back of my garden – OK, basement – flat, there is a narrow patio just big enough to have breakfast on, on a sunny morning, or host a barbecue on a summer's evening. Then beyond a waist-high wall is a bank where daffodils sprout in springtime. As I am not much of gardener, the loose soil there is sown with what my mother calls 'ground cover'. Until recently, it was shaded by a buddleia. At the top of the bank is a metal fence, along which I have tried to train a tree to form a hedge. High trees then obscure the view from the buildings in the next street.

So, if some murderous altercation occurred in my flat one night and I had a corpse to dispose of, I would at least have somewhere to plant it. Being a city-dweller, I don't actually have a spade, of course. And the physical effort of digging even the shallowest grave may be beyond me – certainly in a single night.

But over Christmas, say, when the building is practically deserted and those in residence would have little reason to venture out, it may just about be possible to conceal the evidence of my misdeeds. I fervently hope the opportunity to check this out never arises.

Dear reader, it seems to me that, if there is a possibility that I could get away with it, so could you. So treat the following stories of those who did not succeed in getting away with their evil acts by burying the evidence in the back garden as cautionary tales.

Nigel Cawthorne
Bloomsbury, January 2014

1

THE CORPSE GARDEN

The most notorious case of burying bodies in the back garden in recent years was that of Fred and Rosemary West, who buried the bodies of their victims at their home, 25 Cromwell Street in Gloucester. Indeed, veteran crime writer Colin Wilson's definitive account of the case is called *The Corpse Garden*.

On 24 February 1994, the police turned up at the Wests' ordinary three-storey house in central Gloucester – later to be known as the 'House of Horrors' – with a warrant to dig up the back garden. The door was answered by Stephen West, the 20-year-old son of the householders. The police told him that they were looking for the body of his elder sister Heather, who had disappeared in June 1987 at the age of 16. Stephen's parents had told him that she had left home to go and work in a holiday camp in Devon and he believed that she was now living in the Midlands with her lesbian lover.

'I wanted to know the reasons why they thought Heather was buried there, but they wouldn't tell me,' said Stephen, perhaps disingenuously. At his father's request, Stephen had dug the fish pond that had become Heather's makeshift grave when the patio was extended over it.

Among the surviving West children, there was a running joke that Heather was buried under the patio. Indeed, Fred West himself had threatened them that, if they did not keep quiet about the terrible things that went on in the house, they would end up under the patio like Heather. Nevertheless, Stephen told one of the detectives that they were going to end up making fools of themselves. He replied, 'That's up to us.'

When his mother Rosemary saw the warrant, she said, 'This is stupid.' Then she became hysterical, hurling abuse at the police and claiming they were invading her home. Stephen joined in, demanding that they wait until his father got home. The police told him that they were going to dig up the back garden whether he was there or not.

As the four-man police excavation team trooped out to the rear of the property, Rosemary West tried to contact Fred, who was working on a building site about twenty minutes' drive from Gloucester. She got through to Fred's boss. Sobbing, she said, 'I don't care where he is ... I want him home now.'

Finally, they got through to Fred. 'You'd better get back home,' Rosemary told him. 'They're going to dig up the garden, looking for Heather.'

He said he would leave what he was doing and come

straight home. That was at 1.50pm and they expected him home in 20 minutes. Meanwhile, the police were taking pictures of the back garden. There were concrete slabs to take up and nightfall came at 4.00pm. Not much progress could be made that evening. The excavation team went at 5.30pm, leaving a solitary officer to stand guard all night.

Fred did not arrive home until 5.40pm. It has never been established what he was doing during the intervening four hours. Fred said that he had pulled the lids off some paint pots. The fumes had overcome him as he was driving home and had pulled over into a lay-by where he had passed out. Detective Superintendent John Bennett, who was leading the investigation, believes that Fred West needed 'thinking time'. Others suspected that he was disposing of evidence.

When Rosemary was interviewed, she told the police that Heather had been both lazy and disagreeable, and they were well rid of her. Fred said that she was a lesbian who had got involved in drugs and, like his wife, he seemed unconcerned with her disappearance. 'Lots of girls disappear,' he said, 'take a different name and go into prostitution.' He was more concerned about the mess the police were making raising the paving stones of his patio.

That night, Fred and Rosemary West stayed up all night talking. According to Geoffrey Wansel, author of *Evil Love*, based on 150 hours of taped interviews with Fred West, that night they cooked up a deal. Rosemary was to keep silent, while Fred said that he would sort everything out with the police the following day. She was not to worry about anything as he would take the blame.

In the morning, Stephen found his father staring out of the bathroom window at the garden; the digging had resumed. Fred West's face was contorted and he gave his son a look that sent shivers down his spine. 'I shall be going away for a while,' he said. 'Look after Mum and sell the house. I've done something really bad. I want you to go to the papers and make as much money as you can and start a new life.'

Then Fred presented himself to the officers downstairs and asked to be taken to the police station. As Fred stepped into a police car, he told Detective Constable Hazel Savage, who had instigated the search, that he had killed Heather. He said that her body was buried in the garden, but that the police were digging in the wrong spot. At Gloucester Police Station, Fred told detectives how he had murdered his daughter, cut her body into three pieces and buried them in the back garden, adding, 'The thing I'd like to stress is that Rose knew nothing at all.'

Nevertheless, Rosemary West was arrested on suspicion of being complicit in Heather's murder and taken to Cheltenham Police Station. When she was told of Fred's confession, Rosemary claimed that Fred had sent her out of the house the day Heather disappeared. She had no knowledge of Heather's death.

She was also asked if Fred had mentioned the patio in their conversation the previous evening. 'It had come up,' she admitted. 'We was just waiting for them to do the job and go away again,' she said. 'We hoped they'd put it back the way they found it.'

Twenty minutes after his detailed confession, Fred West retracted everything he had said. 'Heather's alive and well, right,' he insisted. 'She's possibly at the moment in Bahrain working for a drug cartel. She has a Mercedes, a chauffeur and a new birth certificate.'

West was adamant that the police could dig up the back garden as much as they liked, but they would not find Heather.

DS Bennett said that he was surprised how small the garden was for a large Victorian house. It was 25–30ft long and no more that 15–20ft wide, and enclosed by a high wall and trees. Once the concrete slabs had been lifted, a mini-digger was brought in down a pathway to the rear. But when it dug down more than the depth of a spade, they came across a layer of thick, black mud that smelled of sewage. As they dug deeper, this oozed in, filling the hole.

A scene-of-crime tent was brought in to cover the garden. As the excavation team removed the topsoil, they found small bones and bone fragments. A local anthropologist examined them and said they belonged to small animals.

Just below the surface, near the ramshackle extension West had added to the house, they found a larger bone that looked suspiciously human. During his long career with the police force, DS Bennett had come across bones like this before, only to be told they were of Roman origin. But still, it would be checked out.

The fire brigade turned up with a pump to remove the water from the hole that was now surrounded by planks. As the water level dropped, a new smell emanated from the pit. It was adipocere, the smelly, waxy substance that comes from rotting flesh. Bennett had smelt it many times before. Earlier in his career, he had been a police diver and had recovered decomposing bodies. Then the diggers found what looked like human hair.

As the mud was pumped from the hole, the edges began to crumble, but more bones became visible, including a large one that could have come from an arm or a leg. Bennett then called a halt to the excavation and called in the top Home Office pathologist, Professor Bernard Knight.

Bennett put the bone they had found near the extension in an evidence bag and took it back to the station. When Professor Knight arrived, he identified it as a human thighbone – a femur. It came from a young woman aged between 15–25.

Professor Knight arrived in the Wests' back garden at 7.00pm; it was dark and drizzling. He quickly identified the bones in the pit as human. Although the professor had lost his sense of smell many years before, he could see the soapy, grey adipocere in the soil. He began removing the bones and reassembling them. Under the torso, there was a black bin-liner. The head had been separated, although the hair was still in place; the water-sodden soil had preserved it. But no fragments of material were found – no buttons or zips. It was clear that the girl had been buried naked.

When West was told what they had found, he again confessed to murdering his daughter, but it had been an accident, he said. Heather was headstrong; there had been a row; he had slapped her for insolence, but she had simply laughed in his face. So he grabbed her by the throat, but he had gripped her too hard and she stopped breathing. He had tried to resuscitate her, but had no medical training. So he dragged her to the bathroom to douse her with cold water. When this did not revive her, he took her clothes off and dried her. Now he had a corpse to dispose of. He tried putting her body in the large rubbish bin, but it would not fit, so he had to dismember her. First, though, he had to make sure that she was dead, so he strangled her with her tights.

'I didn't want to touch her while she was alive,' said West. 'I mean, if I'd have started cutting her leg or her throat and she'd have suddenly come alive ...'

Before he began his gruesome task, West closed Heather's eyes. According to his own account, he was squeamish. 'If somebody's sat there looking at you, you're not going to use a knife on that person, are you?' he said.

West then gave a detailed description of the process. When he cut off her head, it made a 'horrible noise ... like scrunching'. Cutting her legs off was more problematic. Twisting one of her feet, he heard 'one almighty crack and the leg came loose'.

Once the head and legs had been cut off, the dismembered corpse fitted neatly into the rubbish bin. That night, once everyone had gone to bed, he had buried the body in the back garden. It had lain undiscovered for seven years and that was the end of the story – or so he said.

But it was far from over. Professor Knight had retrieved a

full set of bones from the pit in Fred West's back garden. But the femur found near the extension had to be accounted for. 'Either we've found the world's first three-legged woman,' said Knight, 'or there's another victim around here somewhere.' Clearly, there was more than one body buried in the back garden at 25 Cromwell Street.

When Fred West was interviewed again, he reprised the story of the murder and dismemberment of his daughter at some length.

'Heather didn't have three legs,' said a detective. 'Is there anyone else buried in your garden?'

'Only Heather,' West insisted, falling silent.

After a long pause, he was asked whether he had any idea where the other bone might have come from. There was another long pause and, finally, West said softly, 'Yes ... Shirley.'

'Shirley who?'

'Robinson. The girl that caused the problem.'

According to West, he had had an affair with 18-year-old Shirley Robinson and made her pregnant. She wanted to marry him and was going to tell Rosemary. He could not let that happen, so he strangled her, cut her up and buried her under the patio.

Then West admitted to another murder. The victim this time was 17-year-old Alison Chambers. She was Shirley Robinson's lesbian lover, West said. She had come looking for her. He had told her that Shirley no longer lived there. Alison seemed to accept that, he said, but she came back three weeks later and said she was going to tell the police.

West said he persuaded her not to and offered her a lift back to Bristol. On the way, he stopped in a lay-by and strangled her. Her dismembered body would also be found in the back garden. West had now admitted to having buried three bodies in the back garden. But there was much more to come.

Born in 1941 in the village of Much Marcle, some 14 miles north-west of Gloucester, Fred West was the last of a long line of Herefordshire farm labourers. His parents, Walter and Daisy West, had six children over a ten-year period whom they brought up in rural poverty. Fred had been a beautiful baby with blond hair and piercing blue eyes; he was his mother's favourite. A doting son, he did everything she asked. He also enjoyed a good relationship with his father, whom he regarded as a role model. His father, he said, had liberal ideas when it came to sex. 'If it's on offer, take, son ... that was my father's idea,' he said. 'Whatever you enjoy, do ... only make sure you don't get caught doing it.'

However, as he grew up Fred West lost his childish good looks. His blond hair turned dark brown and curly. He had inherited some of his mother's less attractive features – narrow eyes and a big mouth with a large gap between his front teeth. Some put this down to gypsy blood. Sterner critics called him simian.

Scruffy and unkempt, West did not do well at school. He was a troublesome pupil and was thrashed regularly. His mother, now seriously overweight and always badly dressed, would turn up at his school to remonstrate with the teachers. This led to him being teased as a 'mummy's boy'. He left school at 15, practically illiterate, and went to work, like his father before him, as a farmhand.

By the time he was 16, West had begun to take an interest in girls. He tidied himself up a bit and aggressively pursued any woman who took his fancy. This included close relatives, and he claimed to have made his sister pregnant. He also alleged that his father had committed incest with his daughters. 'I made you so I'm entitled to have you,' West suggests his father said to them. But then, West was a practised liar. He also claimed that his mother had taken him to bed before his 13th birthday. As far as sex was concerned, anything went.

At 17, Fred got a job in a cider factory and bought a motorbike. One night, he ran over a pushbike that had been left in the road and crashed into a brick wall. One leg was broken and was left permanently shorter than the other. A wound to his head took weeks to heal, but he did not have a steel plate surgically inserted as he claimed later. However, after the accident he was prone to sudden fits of rage and seems to have lost control over his emotions.

He spent three years as a seaman and travelled the world, although he avoided dockside prostitutes for fear of sexually transmitted diseases. 'I wasn't paying for it. I got it for nothing,' he said. 'These girls loved it. There were times when I slept with three or four girls twice in the same night, all in the same bed. That's what sex is all about – pleasure.'

Returning to Gloucester, he hooked up with a pretty

16-year-old girl named Catherine Bernadette Costello, nicknamed Rena. A street prostitute in Glasgow from an early age, she had been warned by the police about soliciting at the age of 16. Soon afterwards, she was sent to borstal for attempted burglary. Fleeing her pimp, she came south to Gloucester where she met Fred. The two misfits quickly became lovers, but the relationship was halted when Rena returned home to Scotland a few months later.

Eager for more sex, Fred became ever more forcefully promiscuous. One night while standing on a fire escape outside a local youth club, he stuck his hand up a young woman's skirt. She reacted furiously, knocking him over the balustrade. In the fall, he banged his head again and lost consciousness. This may well have aggravated the frontal lobe damage caused by the motorcycle accident.

Fred West then embarked on a career in petty theft. In 1961, he and a friend stole cigarette cases and a watchstrap from a local jeweller's shop. They were caught red-handed with the stolen goods and were fined. A few months later, he was accused of getting a 13-year-old girl, a friend of the family, pregnant. Fred was unrepentant. He did not see anything wrong in molesting underage girls. 'Doesn't everyone do it?' he said.

He was convicted but, at his trial, West's GP claimed that he suffered from epileptic fits. This saved him from serving a jail sentence but, by the age of 20, Fred West was already a convicted thief and child molester. And he showed no sign of changing his ways. His family threw him out and he went to work on building sites where, again, he was caught stealing. And there were more allegations that he was having sex with underage girls.

West's parents eventually relented and let him return to the family home in Much Marcle. Then, in the summer of 1962, Rena Costello returned from Scotland and took up with Fred again. This time she was pregnant by her pimp. West boasted that during the time he was away at sea he had learnt to perform abortions. He tried it out on her – and failed.

Rena had breached the conditions of her parole and the police caught up with her. To get her out of trouble, Fred proposed – and she accepted. His parents did not approve of the marriage and, at the last minute, Fred got cold feet and offered his brother John £5 to marry her instead. He refused. Nevertheless, Fred went ahead.

His parents would not allow Rena in the house, so the couple moved to Scotland. There, the father of Rena's child, 'a Pakistani who ran a string of corner shops', Fred said, took him on as Rena's 'minder'. There were strict rules about what he could and couldn't do with Rena, although West claimed that the boss let him go with his other girls free of charge. Even so, he began beating Rena.

When Rena's daughter Charmaine was born in March 1963, Fred got Rena to write to his mother, explaining that their baby had died and they had adopted a mixed-race child. West took little interest in the infant and left her with a childminder while he drove Rena to meet her clients. Meanwhile, his interest in straightforward vaginal sex had waned. Instead, he would insist on oral sex, bondage and sodomy at all hours of the day and night.

Rena was not always willing to comply with Fred's urges, but he had easy access to other women and was unfaithful on a daily basis. Their marriage went through a number of rocky patches with frequent separations. But in 1964, Rena gave birth to West's child, Anne-Marie.

West took a job driving an ice-cream truck, and was involved in an accident that resulted in the death of a four-year-old boy. It had not been his fault, but he was concerned that he might lose his job. Around that time, Fred and Rena had met a young Scottish woman named Ann McFall, whose boyfriend had been killed in an accident. Together, the three of them, plus Rena's two children, moved to Gloucester, where West said he began to do the rounds with his old girlfriends again, even claiming to have had sex with one on the altar of a nearby church.

He also became predatory. Thirty years later, one woman recalled being stalked by him when she was sixteen. Another, who accepted a lift from him when hitch-hiking, said he stopped in a lane and told her to remove her knickers. When she refused, he exposed himself. She fled, but he caught up with her and dragged her back to the car with his arm around her throat. Then suddenly he became pleasant and charming. Both women reported him to the police, but no action was taken.

West then got a job in a slaughterhouse. According to Colin Wilson, it was while working there that West developed a morbid obsession with corpses, blood and dismemberment. 'There is no evidence that he had shown any such interest so far,' said Wilson. 'It seems, then, that Fred West's sexual perversion became slowly more obsessive in the period following his marriage, and the evidence suggests that necrophilia and desire to mutilate corpses began during his period as a butcher,' he wrote in *The Corpse Garden*.

West's marriage became increasingly unstable. Rena was repeatedly beaten and fled back to Scotland but Fred refused to let her take the two children with her. Missing her daughters, Rena returned to Gloucester in July 1966 to find Fred and Ann McFall living together in a caravan. Around that time, there had been eight sexual assaults in the area committed by a man answering West's description.

Rena then stole some cigarettes and an iron from another caravan on the site and fled back to Scotland to escape the police. It did not work. She was arrested and 22-year-old PC Hazel Savage, who had joined the Gloucester Constabulary two years earlier, was sent to fetch her. On the way back, Rena told PC Savage about her cruel and perverted husband who was always having affairs and said that she had only resorted to theft to spite him. It was Hazel Savage's first brush with Fred West.

By the beginning of 1967, McFall was pregnant with West's child. Even though she was pregnant, he persuaded her to indulge in bondage. But at six months, fearing for her child, she began to deny him. Nothing made Fred West angrier than a woman who said no. West responded by killing McFall and burying her in Letterbox Field in Much

Marcle, near the caravan site and right behind Moorcourt Cottage, his childhood home.

West not only murdered his lover and their unborn child, he painstakingly dismembered the corpse, removing the foetus, which he buried alongside McFall's body parts – although some were missing. When the corpse was unearthed in 1994, the fingers and toes could not be found. This was to be his hallmark in future crimes. Nevertheless, West went to his death denying that he had killed McFall, repeatedly blaming Rena for Ann's death, although he admitted helping bury her. Again, when Ann's body was found, the hands were tied and a long length of rope was twisted around her arms. This would be another familiar feature in later murders.

Despite her gruesome end, West memorialised her in his handwritten memoir that he wrote in prison in the last days of his life. It is called *I Was Loved by an Angel*. That angel was Ann McFall.

After Ann McFall's disappearance, Rena moved into the caravan with West. With his encouragement, she went to work as a prostitute again. Meanwhile, he began openly molesting four-year-old Charmaine and looked for a nanny who might be persuaded to work as a prostitute with his wife.

On 6 January 1968, pretty 15-year-old Mary Bastholm was abducted from a bus stop in Gloucester. She had been on the way to see her boyfriend and was carrying a Monopoly game. The pieces were found strewn around the bus stop. West always denied abducting Mary Bastholm, but he admitted knowing her. He was a customer at the Pop-In Café, where Mary worked. She had often served him tea when he had been employed to do some building work behind the café. Mary had also been seen with a woman answering the description of Ann McFall. Later, with his second wife Rosemary, he regularly abducted young women from bus stops and one witness claimed to have seen Mary in West's car. West's son Stephen said that, while in jail, his father boasted of killing Bastholm. Her body has never been found.

A month after Mary Bastholm went missing, West's mother died after a routine gallbladder operation and West became seriously unstable. He changed jobs several times and committed a series of petty thefts. Then his life changed. On 29 November 1968, while working as a delivery driver for a local bakery, he met the 15-year-old girl who would become his second wife and would help him dispose of the bodies in the back garden of 25 Cromwell Street.

Rosemary Letts was born in November 1953 in Devon. Her background was disturbed; her father, Bill Letts, was a paranoid schizophrenic. He demanded total obedience from his wife and children, and used violence to get his way. 'If he felt we were in bed too late,' said Rose's brother Andrew, 'he would throw a bucket of cold water over us. He would order us to dig the garden, and that meant the whole garden. Then he would inspect it like an army officer and, if he was not satisfied, we would have to do it all over again.'

A martinet, he enjoyed disciplining his children and was always on the lookout for reasons to beat them. 'We were not allowed to speak and play like normal children,' said Andrew. 'If we were noisy, he would go for us with a belt or chunk of wood.'

His wife Daisy also suffered during these violent outbursts. 'He would beat you black and blue until Mum got in between us,' Andrew said. 'Then she would get a good hiding.'

His savagery and his mental instability did little to recommend him to employers and he drifted through a series of low-paid, unskilled jobs. Short of housekeeping money and in the thrall of a violent husband, Daisy Letts suffered from severe depression. She had already given birth to three daughters and a son when she was hospitalised in 1953 and given electroshock therapy (now referred to as electroconvulsive therapy). At the time, she was pregnant with Rosemary and it is thought that these shocks could have had an effect on the child's development in her mother's womb.

Rosemary was noticeably different from the other Letts' children. In her cot, she developed the habit of rocking violently. As she grew older, she rocked only her head – but for hours on end as if she was in a trance. The family soon realised that she was a bit slow. They called her 'Dozy Rosie'. However, with big brown eyes and a clear complexion, she was a pretty child. This appealed to her father and, by doing everything he asked without question, she became the apple of his eye and escaped the beatings he meted out to her siblings. In return, she endured repeated sexual abuse from him.

Bill Letts's father, Walter, was also a paedophile who may have abused his granddaughter, too. This pattern of abuse was handed down a generation. Once, when Bill Letts visited the Wests' house, Anne-Marie came downstairs complaining that 'grampy' was trying to get into bed with her. Rosemary ordered her to go back upstairs and get on with it.

Things did not go well for Rosemary at school. With no appreciable intellectual gifts, she struggled academically. As she grew older, she developed a tendency towards chubbiness and was teased relentlessly. In response, she lashed out.

As an adolescent, Rose became precocious sexually. After taking a bath, she would walk around the house naked. Her father forbade her to go out with boys her own age. Not that many were interested. Both her reputation as an ill-tempered, sullen, aggressive loner and her chubbiness put the local boys off. Instead, she concentrated on the older men in the village.

After 15-year-old Mary Bastholm disappeared in January 1968, most girls in the Gloucester area were on their guard. But Rosemary's growing interest in sex meant that she would not stay at home and, on one occasion, one of the older men she was dating raped her.

At the beginning of 1969, Daisy Letts left and moved in temporarily with her older daughter, Glenys, and her husband, Jim Tyler. Freed from her father's strictures, the

15-year-old Rose spent all her time going out. Her brother-in-law said that Rose carried on with numerous older men and that she had even tried to seduce him. After a few months, to everyone's surprise, Daisy moved back to Bill, taking Rose with her. It was then that Rose met 28-year-old Fred West.

West wanted her to be his sex slave – a role that she had been trained for by her father. She was prepared to do anything to satisfy his perverted desires. However compliant she may have been, though, Rosemary Letts was not the only woman in West's life at the time. He was always on the lookout for young women he could take home for the night. One evening, he persuaded a young couple to come back to the caravan. There, West again boasted about his abilities as an abortionist, suggesting his services if they ever got into trouble. He showed them a hideous corkscrew device he said he used and a pack of Polaroid pictures of the vaginas of girls he said he had operated on.

Whatever Bill Letts's shortcomings as a parent, he tried to keep his underage daughter away from West. When Bill discovered that Rose was having sex with West, he reported him to the Social Services. This proved ineffective, so Bill turned up at West's caravan and threatened him. The relationship was halted briefly when West went to prison for theft and failure to pay fines. But Rose was already pregnant with West's child. At 16, she left her father's house and moved into a flat West had rented to take care of Rena's two daughters.

In 1970, Rose gave birth to the ill-fated Heather. With Fred in jail, no money and three children to take care of, the teenage Rose found it hard to cope. Her temper flared constantly. She particularly resented having to rear another woman's children and treated Charmaine and Anne-Marie abominably.

In the summer of 1971, eight-year-old Charmaine went missing. Rose told her sister Anne-Marie that their mother Rena had come to get her. There is no doubt that Rose killed her. In *The Corpse Garden*, Colin Wilson thinks that Rose 'simply lost her temper, and went further than usual in beating or throttling her. She was, as Anne-Marie said, a woman entirely without self-control; when she lost her temper, she became a kind of maniac.'

At Rose West's trial, the prosecution claimed that she had killed Charmaine in a fit of anger and dumped the body in the coal cellar until Fred returned from prison to dispose of the corpse. He buried the body under the kitchen floor. The flat had no garden. When the body was found, the fingers and toes were missing, just as Anna McFall's had been.

In August 1971, Rena came to look for her daughter. Unable to get any sense out of Fred or Rose, Rena visited Fred's father, Walter, hoping he could shed some light on what had happened to Charmaine, intimating that she might go to the police. 'My father and Rena were close,' West said. 'Whether the old man was having an affair with her I don't know.'

Fred West maintained that Rena went voluntarily to a

romantic spot in Letterbox Field in a car belonging to the pimp that he used to collect clients for Rosemary. After they made love against an oak tree, West said, they had a row, which ended with him kicking her to death. He happened to have a 2½ ft-long Jamaican sabre knife with him to cut her up, along with a pickaxe and spade to bury her not far from Ann McFall. Like Ann, Rena was buried naked and a number of bones were missing, including those of her fingers and toes.

Fred and Rosemary maintained for almost a quarter of a century that Rena and Charmaine had gone off to Scotland together to start a new life. But after he was arrested, West insisted that Rosemary had murdered Rena in the flat at Midland Road and that the pimp had cut her up. The dismembered body, he said, had been left in plastic bags in a garage. After he found it, he helped them to bury her.

However it had actually happened, Fred and Rose were now bound together by murder. Later, when Rose's father came to take her away, West said, 'Come on, Rosie, you know what we've got between us.'

This upset Rose, Bill Letts noted. Afterwards, Rosemary told her parents why she could not leave, saying, 'You don't know him. There's nothing he wouldn't do – even murder.'

In the 1960s, a large number of West Indian immigrants had come to Gloucester. They were largely single men and Rose invited many of them over to the flat for sex – both for fun and to earn a little extra money. Fred encouraged this. He was a voyeur and enjoyed watching her have sex through a peephole. He later rigged up a speaker system so that he could hear Rosemary's groans while he was watching TV. Even the children could not disturb him while this was going on. Although oversexed, Fred would only join in if the sex involved bondage, sadism, lesbianism or vibrators. He also took suggestive pictures of Rose, using them in advertisements in magazines for 'swingers' and other publications where he advertised her services as a prostitute.

Fred and Rose began employing their neighbour, 19-year-old Elizabeth Agius, as a babysitter. On more than one occasion, when the Wests returned home, Elizabeth asked them where they had been. They said they had been cruising around looking for young girls, preferably virgins. Fred explained that he had taken Rose along, so then they would not be afraid to get into the car with him. Elizabeth thought they were joking. Rosemary admitted that she was a prostitute and invited Elizabeth to go to bed with her and Fred, while Fred propositioned her with an eye to bondage. She refused both offers. But later, according to a police statement, she was drugged and came to be naked in bed with Fred and Rosemary.

In January 1972, Fred and Rose married at Gloucester Register Office. And in June, they had another daughter whom they named Mae. They decided they needed a bigger house to raise their growing family and accommodate Rose's prostitution business. One of Rosemary's clients lent them the deposit and they moved into 25 Cromwell Street; it had a garage and a spacious cellar. Frank as ever, Fred told Elizabeth Agius that he planned to convert the cellar into a room where Rose could entertain her clients, or he would soundproof it and turn it into his 'torture chamber'. And this was what he did.

Its first inmate was his own eight-year-old daughter, Anne-Marie. He told her that he and Rose were such caring parents that they were going to teach her how to satisfy her husband when she got married. They stripped and gagged her. Her hands were tied behind her back and Rose held her down while Fred raped her. This hurt her so much that Anne-Marie could not go to school for several days. She was warned not to tell anyone, otherwise she would be beaten. The rapes continued. On one occasion, she was strapped down so her father could rape her quickly during his lunch hour.

Fred and Rose continued cruising the vicinity, looking for young girls. At the end of 1972, they picked up 17-year-old Caroline Raine, who was hitch-hiking. They hired her as a live-in nanny, promising her family that they would take care of her. Caroline was very attractive, and Fred and Rose both tried to seduce her. She found them repellent and, after six weeks, quit. A few days later, they spotted her hitch-hiking again and offered her a lift. In the back of the car, Rosemary started molesting her. When she objected, Fred knocked her unconscious.

He drove them back to Cromwell Street where they stripped her, tied her up, tortured and raped her. Fred threatened that if she told anyone about it, 'I'll keep you in the cellar and let my black friends have you. And when we're finished, we'll kill you and bury you under the paving stones of Gloucester. There are hundreds of girls buried under there.'

Under duress, Caroline agreed to stay on with them. Fred then untied her and let her have a bath. Later, when she went to the launderette with Rosemary, she seized the chance to make a run for it. It was not until the following evening that she plucked up the courage to tell her mother what had happened, and this lady then called the police.

The Wests were arrested. They agreed to plead guilty to indecent assault and actual bodily harm if the charge of rape was dropped. When the matter came to court in January 1973, West was able to convince the magistrate that Caroline had consented to sex. Despite West's long criminal record, they got off with a small fine. By this time, Fred was 31; Rose was 19 and pregnant for the third time. Again, when he was finally caught after the bodies had been found in the back garden, Fred blamed Rosemary for the assault on Caroline Raine.

The Wests began to take in lodgers. One of them had a girlfriend, 19-year-old Lynda Gough, whom Rosemary seduced. Lynda then wanted to move in, so the Wests took her on as a nanny. Fred West claimed that she was into black magic and bizarre sex, and willingly entered into bondage sessions in the basement. But then she found herself locked in the cellar, being tortured and abused for days on end, before she was finally killed. Her fingers and toes were almost certainly cut off while she was still alive and conscious. Bound, gagged and blindfolded, she could not protest. Her hands and wrists were severed shortly after. Her kneecaps, breastbone and seven ribs were also removed.

West maintained that she had been strangled accidentally when he went to answer the front door in the middle of a bondage session. Nevertheless, he had sex with her lifeless body. Then he cut her up and buried her dismembered body under the floor of the garage at the back of the house. Rosemary took her clothes, washed them and wore them.

When Lynda's family asked what had happened to her, they were told she had moved on ... but they noted at the time that Rosemary was wearing something that belonged to their daughter. The other lodgers were told that Lynda had been fired for hitting one of the children. The police were not called and there were no repercussions. Soon after, in August 1973, the West's first son, Stephen, was born.

Having got away with so much, the Wests began killing just for the fun of it. In November 1973, the dismembered body of 15-year-old schoolgirl Carol Ann 'Caz' Cooper was buried under the floor of the cellar in Cromwell Street. It is not known who picked her up or how she died – although it was probably in one of the Wests' torture sessions where the victim was suspended from a beam in the basement. When the body was discovered, the head was bound with surgical tape, so she could neither see nor hear. Fifty of her bones were missing, including most of the bones of the wrists and thirty-five of the bones of the fingers and toes.

The following month, 21-year-old university student Lucy Partington arrived at her mother's house in Gretton near Cheltenham where she was to spend the Christmas holidays. She was the cousin of novelist Martin Amis. On 27 December, she went to visit a disabled friend. She left to catch a bus shortly after 10.00pm and was last seen at a bus stop on the outskirts of Cheltenham.

West claimed that he had known Lucy for some months before she disappeared and they made love in Cheltenham's Pittville Park nearby. She fell pregnant and was going to tell Rosemary, so he strangled her in his van. This was an unlikely tale as Lucy was studying in Exeter and spent little time in Gloucester, so this was one of several implausible stories he'd tell about her.

The most likely scenario is that Rosemary was in the car with Fred when they offered Lucy a lift. It is almost certain that she would not have got into the car if Rose had not been there. The Wests took her back to Cromwell Street where they raped and tortured her for about a week, then murdered her, dismembered her body and buried it under the house.

Fred cut himself while dismembering Lucy's corpse and went to the hospital to have the wound stitched on 3 January 1974. By then, Lucy – like Carol Ann Cooper – had been reported missing, but there was nothing to connect either of the girls to the Wests. Their bodies were concealed in Fred's home improvement scheme. This involved enlarging the cellar and turning the garage into an extension of the main house. The only thing remotely suspicious about this was that Fred's home improvements were done at strange hours of the night. However, West did attract police attention. To pay for his home improvements – and the concrete he covered the corpses with – he committed a series of thefts and fenced stolen goods.

Three more young women – 15-year-old schoolgirl Shirley Hubbard, 19-year-old Juanita Mott from Newent in Gloucestershire and 21-year-old Swiss hitch-hiker Therese Siegenthaler – also ended up under the cellar floor at 25 Cromwell Street. They had been tortured and dis-membered. The Wests had subjected them to extreme bondage, using plastic washing lines and ropes to suspend them from one of the beams in the cellar, and gagging them with tights, nylon socks and a bra. Shirley's head had been completely encased in tape with a plastic tube up her nose to allow her to breathe. Juanita had been gagged with a bra, two pairs of tights and two of Rose West's long, white nylon socks. Then she had been trussed up with plastic-covered washing line. This looped around her wrists and ankles, her arms and thighs, and her head, so that she was completely immobilised. A 7ft length of rope with a slipknot at the end to form a noose was also found with her body. This was thought to have been used to suspend the terrified girl from one of the overhead beams.

In the spring of 1977, Rosemary enticed a young woman from a local home for wayward girls back to Cromwell Street. Being underage, the court called her Miss A. At Number 25, she was fondled by Rosemary before being taken to a bedroom where two naked underage girls were being held prisoner. Miss A was then stripped as well. Once

Rosemary was naked, Fred trussed one of the girls up with parcel tape and Rosemary abused her with a vibrator.

'Are you enjoying this, Fred?' said Rosemary. 'Is it turning you on?'

West then raped the girl.

Rosemary then bound Miss A with tape and abused her with what felt like a candle, while Fred masturbated. He then raped her. Afterwards, she was freed and went to the bathroom with her dress. She put it on and fled the house barefoot, but was too ashamed to tell anyone what had happened at the time.

It is likely that one of the girls held in the bedroom was Anne-Marie, Fred's daughter, who was the regular target of the couple's sexual sadism. But Fred West not only raped and tortured his own daughter, he brought home other men to have sex with her.

Fred had extensively remodelled the house. Upstairs, he had constructed extra bedrooms for the lodgers. One of them was 18-year-old Shirley Robinson. A former prostitute with bisexual inclinations, she had sex with both Rose and Fred.

Rose fell pregnant by one of her West Indian clients and gave birth to Tara in December 1977. At the time, Shirley was also pregnant, carrying Fred's child. Rose was unhappy about this; she feared that Shirley would displace her in Fred's affections. So she had to go. In July 1978, Shirley Robinson was strangled. By this time, the cellar was full, so Shirley and her unborn child became the first to be buried in the back garden at 25 Cromwell Street.

In November 1978, Rose gave birth to another daughter. She was Fred's child and they named her Louise. There were now six children in the household and, from an early age, they were aware of what was going on. They knew that Rose was a prostitute and that Anne-Marie was being sexually abused by her father. Anne-Marie eventually fell pregnant by Fred, but it was an ectopic pregnancy and had to be aborted. She then moved out to live with her boyfriend, so Fred turned his sexual attentions towards Heather. Heather tried to resist and was beaten.

Not even the loss of Rose's father in May 1979 disturbed the Wests' gruesome activities. Several months later, a troubled 16-year-old from Swansea named Alison Chambers began to visit. Twenty-five Cromwell Street appeared to be a haven away from the children's home that she loathed. Other girls from the children's home also visited and the Wests encouraged them to make extra money as part-time prostitutes. One recalled being tied to a slab in a satanic ritual where she was raped by Fred West as eight men looked on.

Alison Chambers soon featured in both the Wests' sex lives. On 4 August 1979, she decided to run away from the children's home. It was clear that she intended to live in Cromwell Street although her friends were to tell the staff that she had run away to Wales. She was supposed to meet her friends the next day to collect some clothes she had left behind. She did not turn up and the following day the police were informed. However, in September, her mother received a letter from her saying she was living with a 'very homely family' and looking after their five children. This was enough to persuade the social services that she was not a missing person. The letter betrayed no sense of danger. Nothing is known of what happened to Alison until her thighbone was unearthed from under the patio at 25 Cromwell Street years later.

West said that they had had a row; he had punched her, then strangled her with his bare hands. Later, he said he had strangled her with a piece of electrical cable to make sure she was dead. Then he had buried her under the paddling pool, afterwards explaining that he could not make a hole big enough without a sledgehammer, so he had to cut her head and legs off. However, she was naked when she was buried and had clearly been subjected to some sort of sexual abuse.

In June 1980, Rose gave birth to Fred's second son, Barry. In April 1982, Rose had Rosemary Junior, who was not Fred's child. Then in July 1983, Rose had yet another daughter, Lucyanna. Like Tara and Rosemary Junior, she was mixed race. It is thought that the Wests kept on carrying out sexual abductions throughout this period but, as they did not bury any of the victims at 25 Cromwell Street and refused to confess to any murders during the early 1980s, one cannot be sure.

Having eight children in the household took its toll on Rose's temper. She became increasingly irrational and beat them without provocation. This began to loosen the children's bond of loyalty. Their continued silence was the Wests' only protection.

In June 1987, Heather, who was then 16, decided that

she would resist her father's sexual demands. At the time, Rosemary was also showing a sexual interest in Heather, with Fred's encouragement. In a fit of pique, Heather challenged her mother and father about the parentage of her three mixed-race sisters. Her father had claimed they were a throwback to his 'gypsy past'. To Heather, though, it was clear that they were the children of one of her mother's West Indian clients and she confronted one of the other daughters of that particular man.

In Fred and Rosemary's eyes, she had overstepped the mark, talking to someone outside the family about their business. She received a tremendous beating. They then waited until the end of the school year, so there would be no awkward questions from teachers, before they strangled her. The other children were told that she had left home, while Fred and Rosemary played an elaborate charade with telephone calls and supposed sightings to make them believe she was alive and well. Acquaintances were told that she had run off with a lesbian lover.

Fred asked his 13-year-old son Stephen to help him dig a hole in the back garden. Later, Fred buried Heather's dismembered body there. Afterwards, slabs were laid over it. When her body was eventually recovered from under the patio, it was clear that she had been treated in the same way as the other victims; she had been decapitated, dismembered and disarticulated, and a number of bones were missing. Two lengths of orange cord of the type that Fred carried in his van to tie ladders to the roof were found. One was entangled in her hair.

Fred West could barely bring himself later to look at the anatomical drawings showing which bones were missing. When asked whether any of these parts of the body had been removed while Heather was alive, he said, 'I've no comment on that.'

Twenty-two of the twenty-six bones in the fingers and toes were missing, along with fifteen from her wrists and ankles. Her right kneecap was also absent. Her right thigh had been smashed with a meat cleaver and the legs disarticulated from the pelvis with a sharp knife. West maintained that he had killed his daughter in a simple disagreement about leaving home.

Over the next few weeks, Fred and Rosemary extended the patio out over the garden. Stephen was surprised to see the hole that he had been digging for a new paddling pool and been filled in and covered over.

In the years that followed, the other children tried to locate their missing sister. The older siblings filled out a Salvation Army missing-persons form. But when they talked about reporting her missing to the police, they were told that Heather had been involved in credit card fraud and that, if they went to the police, they would get her into trouble.

When divorcée Katherine Halliday moved into 11 Cromwell Street, Fred invited her round to meet Rosemary. Immediately, she was treated to a pornographic video. Rosemary sat next to her. She was wearing a miniskirt and a low-cut top – and no underwear. Halliday was then dragged up to the bedroom where both Rosemary and Fred had sex with her. After that, she and Rosemary became regular lovers, with Fred usually watching. The sex quickly became more aggressive, with Fred showing her amateur videos he had probably made himself featuring increasingly violent sado-masochism.

The levels of bondage Halliday underwent were then stepped up. She noted that the Wests liked to see her frightened, but when they showed her rubber suits and masks that had no holes for the nose and mouth, she got so scared that she did not go back again.

The Wests' campaign of rape and murder had been going on for 20 years, but only now did they begin to run out of luck. When Fred began raping one of his younger daughters and videoing it, she told one of her school friends. And another one of the very young girls they had abducted and raped also told a girlfriend what happened. The girl went to the police and the case was assigned to the newly promoted DC Hazel Savage.

On 6 August 1992, the police arrived at 25 Cromwell Street with a search warrant. They were looking for evidence of child abuse, and found a mountain of distasteful pornography; both Fred and Rosemary were arrested. Fred was charged with the rape and sodomy of a minor and Rose was charged with assisting him.

Hazel Savage was assigned to the case. She knew of Fred from 1966 when Rena had told her about his sexual perversions, and she set about interviewing the Wests' friends and family members. Anne-Marie talked openly about the abuse she had suffered at Fred's hands. She also expressed her suspicions about the fate of Charmaine, whom DC Savage had known from her investigations in 1966. Rena, it seemed, had also gone missing. Savage checked tax and national insurance records which showed that Heather had not been employed, drawn benefits or visited a doctor in five years. Either she had moved abroad or she was dead.

The younger children were taken into care. Unable to cope without Fred, who remained in custody, Rosemary tried to kill herself by taking an overdose of pills. But her son Stephen found her in time and saved her life. In jail, Fred became self-pitying and depressed. But still his luck held. The case against him collapsed when two key witnesses decided not to testify against them and he was released.

However, DC Savage now launched an inquiry into the whereabouts of Heather. The West children joked that she was under the patio; they said that Fred had threatened them that if they did not keep their mouths shut about the goings-on at 25 Cromwell Street they would end up under the patio like Heather.

The task was daunting. Digging up a 600sq-ft garden was a huge undertaking and was bound to attract media attention, especially since the extension to the house had been built over part of the garden. But DS John Bennett eventually got a warrant.

After the discovery of the bones in the garden, Fred West was charged with the murder of Heather West, Shirley Robinson and an unidentified third woman, who turned out to be Alison Chambers. To protect Rose, Fred took full responsibility for the murders.

The police now broadened the investigation to look into the disappearance of Rena and Charmaine. Fred was assigned an 'appropriate adult' named Janet Leach. She was usually assigned to befriend and assist juveniles or the mentally subnormal when they were taken into custody. Fred West was thought to fall into this second category. Leach asked Fred whether there were any more bodies. West admitted that there were and sketched a map of the cellar and bathroom, showing where six more bodies lay. He admitted to murdering the girls he had buried there, but not to raping them. The girls, he insisted, had wanted to have sex with him. However, he did not even know the names of some of his victims. He called Carol Ann Cooper simply 'Scar Hand' because of a burn on her hand caused by a firework. Thérèse Siegenthaler he referred to as 'Tulip' under the mistaken impression that she was Dutch; she was Swiss. This made it difficult for the police to identify the bodies. With large numbers of people being reported missing each year, it was a mammoth task to match a set of remains to a missing person's report.

Of course, Fred West did know the names of some of his victims. He admitted to murdering his first wife Rena and his lover Ann McFall and burying their bodies in the fields near Much Marcle. He also admitted to the murder of Charmaine, Rena's eldest daughter. With his help, the bodies of Rena, Ann McFall and Charmaine were found. However, he refused to co-operate over the disappearance of Mary Bastholm and her body has never been located.

From the start, the police were convinced that Rose West was involved in the murders, even though she feigned shock at her husband's confessions and denied everything. She played the naïve and innocent victim of a murderous and manipulative man. Along with Stephen and her eldest daughter Mae, she was moved by the police into a safe house in Cheltenham. The house was bugged by police, but Rose never said anything which implicated herself. However, on 18 April 1994, she was charged with a sex offence and taken into custody. The murder charges would come later.

By this time, the world's media had turned up in Gloucester. There were TV crews from America and Japanese film interviews in the street. Journalists quickly dubbed 25 Cromwell Street the 'House of Horrors'. The fact that a serial killer had been operating in Gloucester for over 25 years came as a shock to its citizens. They had got away with it because, with the exception of Lucy Partington, the Wests had deliberately targeted people who drifted in and out of society and whose disappearance would not be noticed. Nevertheless, the international attention the Wests had brought the city came as a terrible blow to Gloucester's civic pride.

On 13 December 1994, Fred West was charged with 12 murders. He and Rose appeared together in court. In the dock, Fred tried to comfort Rose, but she pulled away from him, telling the police that he made her sick. Fred found the rejection devastating. He wrote to her, saying, 'We will always be in love ... You will always be Mrs West, all over the world. That is important to me and to you.' She did not respond.

Just before noon on New Year's Day 1995 at Winson Green Prison in Birmingham, 54-year-old Fred West hanged himself with strips of bed sheet. He had picked his moment well; the guards were at lunch and he had clearly planned his suicide so that he would not be discovered and resuscitated.

This left Rose alone to face ten counts of murder when her trial began on 3 October 1995. Clearly, she could not have been involved in the murder of Rena and Ann McFall as they had been killed before she knew Fred. However, there was little direct evidence to link her to the other murders. Instead, the prosecution, led by Brian Leveson QC, aimed to construct a tight web of circumstantial evidence to prove Rose's guilt.

A number of key witnesses – including Caroline Raine and Miss A – testified to Rose's sadistic assaults on young women. The prosecution maintained that the abduction of Caroline Raine was a blueprint for how the Wests picked up their victims. Caroline escaped with her life and the Wests were prosecuted and fined over the incident. From then on, it was clear that Fred and Rosemary West had made up their minds that future victims would not be allowed to live to tell the tale.

Fred's confidante Janet Leach also gave crucial evidence. She testified that Fred had told her privately that Rose was involved in the murders – and that Rose had murdered Charmaine and Shirley Robinson by herself. However, West had apparently said that he made a deal with Rose to take all the blame himself. At the time, this confession, given in confidence, had put Ms Leach under so much stress that she suffered a stroke. It was only after Fred's suicide that she felt the bond of confidentiality had been lifted and she told the police what he had revealed to her. Giving testimony, she again was put under enormous stress. She collapsed and had to be taken to hospital, with the trial being adjourned for several days.

The most damning evidence came from Anne-Marie West, who fixed her stepmother with a withering stare as she described how she and Fred had embarked on a campaign of sexual abuse against her when she was eight.

The defence, led by Richard Ferguson QC, maintained that evidence of sexual assault was not the same thing as evidence of murder. He made the case that Rose did not know that Fred was murdering the girls they had abused and burying them around the house and in the back garden. Ferguson then put Rose on the witness stand. She did not impress the jury. The prosecution rattled her by making her angry; she appeared obstructive and defiant. The prosecution also managed to force her to confess to the extent of her maltreatment of the children and she gave the general impression of being unscrupulous and dishonest.

The defence played taped interviews with Fred West, where he said that he had murdered his victims when Rose was out of the house. But it was not difficult for the prosecution to show that Fred was an inveterate liar, so everything he said was open to doubt.

In his closing speech, Leveson maintained that Rose had been the dominant force in the Wests' murderous partnership. She was, he told the jury, the 'strategist'. 'The evidence that Rosemary West knew nothing is not worthy of belief,' he said.

Ferguson, closing for the defence, maintained that the evidence for murder only pointed to Fred. There was no proof that Rose had known anything, let alone participated. The jury did not agree with him; they quickly came to the unanimous verdict that Rosemary West was guilty of the murders of Charmaine West, Heather West, Shirley Robinson and the other girls buried at the house. The judge sentenced Rose to life imprisonment on each of the ten counts of murder. In 1996, her request for leave to appeal was turned down. Home Secretary David Blunkett later told Rosemary West that she would never be released.

In October 1996, Gloucester City Council demolished 25 Cromwell Street. There were calls to create a memorial garden on the site, but there were fears that it would be turned into a ghoulish shrine, so it was left as a landscaped footpath leading to the city centre.

Four years after Rose West was sentenced, her son Stephen revealed that not only had his father admitted killing 15-year-old waitress Mary Bastholm when visiting his father in prison shortly before he died, he had boasted that Bastholm's body would never be found. Stephen said his father had told him, 'I will never tell anyone where she is.' He also talked of a number of other victims and crowed, 'They are not going to find them all, you know, never.'

However, to the police, West had continued strenuously denying that he had killed Bastholm, although she had been seen in his car. Mary Bastholm's brother Peter said he was relieved when he heard what Stephen West had said, although his parents had both died without learning the fate of their only daughter.

In December 1998, Gordon Burn, the author of *Happy Like Murderers*, another book about the Wests, claimed that the bones removed from the victims' bodies – usually fingers and toes, but in some cases kneecaps and entire shoulder blades – had been buried near Pittville Park in Cheltenham, close to the bus stop where Fred first met Rose in 1970. Burns said that the location held an 'almost spiritual' significance for the Wests.

In 2000, Rosemary West secured legal aid to launch a new appeal. Her lawyer, Leo Goatley, said that there was 'new photographic evidence, which would prove that her husband, Fred West, was the sole killer'. The hope was that she would 'be cleared by anatomical photographs of women which were taken by Fred West and seized by police during an earlier investigation in 1992'. The photographs, he asserted, were time stamped and would help his client prove she was not present at the time. The originals, he said, had been destroyed, but Goatley was confident that 'copies would have been made or details of the photographs chronicled by police'. He also said that excessive publicity and chequebook journalism had prevented her from receiving a fair trial, and an application was made to the Criminal Cases Review Commission on 20 October 2000.

But the application was doomed to failure when a TV documentary aired an interview with Janet Leach who revealed that Fred West had confessed to killing many more than the 12 victims he had been charged with murdering. 'Fred said that there were two other bodies in shallow graves in the woods but there was no way they would ever be found,' she told the interviewer. 'He said there were 20 other bodies, not in one place but spread around and he would give police one a year. He told me the truth about the girls in the cellar and what happened to them so I don't see why he would lie about other bodies.'

She also said that West had confessed to the murder of Mary Bastholm. She was one of two young woman 'in shallow graves in the woods, but there was no way they would ever be found'.

'No one has even scratched the surface of this case,' said the documentary's producer. 'Social services had 300 missing files and 100 missing girls. There were two girls from Jordan's Brook Children's Home who were making a living as prostitutes from 25 Cromwell Street.'

The programme also described how West had told his solicitor that he believed the spirits of his victims rose from their graves. 'When they come up into you it's beautiful,' West is alleged to have said. 'It's when they go away you are trying to hold them, you feel them flying away from you and you try to stop them. You can't send them back to where they were.'

Soon after this, Rosemary West abandoned her appeal and told the press that she had resigned herself to spending the rest of her life in Durham's high-security prison. In 2008, she was transferred to the all-women prison at Low Newton in County Durham where she has a private room, complete with a TV, radio, CD player and her own bathroom. She listens to *The Archers* and Neil Diamond, plays Monopoly, cooks and has beauty products from Avon and trinkets from Argos delivered. Among the other inmates in her unit is Tracey Connelly, mother of Baby P, with whom she has struck up a close relationship.

2

THE VEGETABLE PATCH AT RILLINGTON PLACE

John Reginald Christie, the notorious necrophile murderer of 10 Rillington Place, also buried bodies in the back garden. This was discovered after Christie had moved out of the slum property in north Kensington.

Christie had shared the cramped Victorian house with Jamaican-born Beresford Brown and his wife, and other tenants. There was a flat on each of the three storeys. The address was already famous for the 1949 murder of 19-year-old Beryl Evans and her baby daughter Geraldine. Beryl's husband Timothy was hanged for their murder the following year. The Browns had moved into the Evans's top floor once it became vacant.

In March 1953, Christie quit Rillington Place. He had sub-let his ground-floor flat to a Mr and Mrs Reilly, saying that he was moving to Birmingham. His wife, he said, had gone on ahead. When the landlord found out that

Christie had illegally rented the place to sub-tenants, he told them to move out and gave the Browns permission to use the downstairs kitchen. There was no possibility of using the rest of the flat and Christie had left behind piles of rubbish.

Over the next few days, Brown began to tidy the place up, dumping armfuls of old clothes and other rubbish beside an old washhouse in the back garden. Then he began work on the kitchen. First, he wanted to put up a bracket to hold a radio set so he could listen to music while he worked. He tapped what he took to be the back wall and found it was hollow. When he stripped away the wallpaper, he found no wall there at all. It was merely the door to an alcove that had been papered over.

When he opened the door and shone his torch through the crack, he could not believe what he was seeing. Dropping the torch, he ran to the second floor to fetch Ivan Williams, the tenant who lived there. Together, they went back downstairs; Brown then picked up the torch and shone it into the alcove.

They saw a shocking sight. Sitting on top of a pile of rubbish was a partially clothed woman's body. She was wearing a white, cotton pique jacket fastened with a safety pin, a blue bra, stockings and a pink suspender belt. Brown ran to get the police.

When detectives arrived at 10 Rillington Place, they found not just one body in the alcove, but three. A second was wrapped in a blanket attached to the first by the bra straps. Behind them was a third, covered in the same way (an old woollen one), tied at the ankles with some plastic flex. All three women had been strangled.

By the early hours of the next morning, 25 March, the body of a fourth woman was found under the floorboards in the front room. She was identified as Christie's wife Ethel. The police called a halt for the night. An officer was posted outside the house; a guard would remain there for the next few weeks.

The following day, detectives started digging up the tiny back garden at Rillington Place, where Christie grew runner beans. They found the skeletons of two more women. Medical tests showed that they had been buried for approximately ten years. Leading pathologist Dr Francis Camps said that both had been strangled. The skull of one woman was missing.

In the press, Scotland Yard announced that this was 'the most brutal mass killing known in London'. They wanted to interview one 'vital witness' named John Reginald Halliday Christie, and they issued the description of a slight, balding, middle-aged man. Football crowds were asked to report any sighting at once, and Christie's face appeared in every national newspaper. It seemed incredible that another series of murders had occurred at the same address where Timothy Evans had killed his wife only four years before.

John Reginald Christie was born on 8 April 1898 in Black Boy House, Halifax. His father, Ernest, was a pillar of society; a designer for Crossley Carpets, he was also a founder member of the Halifax Conservative Party and a leader of the Primrose League, an organisation promoting purity among the working classes. He was also the first superintendent of the Halifax branch of the St John Ambulance.

Christie's mother Mary was known as 'Beauty Halliday' before her marriage. She was keen on amateur dramatics.

One of seven children, John was his mother's favourite. He was terrified of his disciplinarian father. 'We almost had to ask if we could speak to him,' he wrote later. But Christie had another problem in the family – he found himself completely dominated by his older sisters.

Christie was a good pupil at school and sang in the choir. After school hours, he was a Boy Scout and later became an assistant Scout Master. When he was eight, his maternal grandfather died. Christie felt the trembling sensation of both fascination and pleasure at seeing the body.

After leaving school, Christie started work at the Gem Cinema in Halifax. One day, he and some friends went down the local lovers' lane known as the 'Monkey Run'. They paired off. Christie found himself with a girl much more experienced than him. Intimidated by her, he could not perform. Word got round and his friends started taunting him as 'Reggie-No-Dick' or 'Can't-Do-It-Reggie'.

At 17, Christie was caught stealing and was sacked. His father banned him from the house; he had to sleep on the allotment and his mother would take him food.

He drifted from job to job until he was called up for service in the First World War. Sent to France, he was gassed and was sent home with a disability pension.

On 20 May 1920, he married the long-suffering Ethel

Waddington. The following year, working as a postman, he was caught stealing money from letters and was jailed for nine months. Two years later, he was bound over for posing as an ex-officer and the court put him on probation for violence. Probation did not help; the following year, he served another nine months for theft. His wife then left him.

In 1929, he was sentenced to six months' hard labour for attacking a prostitute and, after yet another spell in prison for stealing a car from a Roman Catholic priest who had befriended him, Christie wrote to Ethel, asking her to have him back. Foolishly, she did.

They moved to London. When they visited Ethel's family in Leeds, Christie spoke of his 'big house in London' with servants. But he never earned over £8 a week, the going rate for a junior clerk. They lived in a shabby little flat in north Kensington and there were no servants.

Just before the outbreak of the Second World War in 1939, Christie became a Special Constable. He seemed to be a reformed character, but he was never popular. Locals feared his petty-mindedness. Christie and another unpopular Special Constable were known as 'the rat and the weasel'.

Although he was losing his hair, Christie still saw himself as a charmer, but his basic hatred of women was plain. 'Women who give you the come-on wouldn't look nearly so saucy if they were helpless and dead,' he said. Christie took pride in concealing his violent intentions from the women he took back to 10 Rillington Place, until it was too late.

BODIES IN THE BACK GARDEN

His first victim was Austrian-born Ruth Fuerst. She worked in a munitions factory, but the pay was poor and she supplemented her income with a little prostitution.

Christie met her while trying to trace a man wanted for theft. She asked him to lend her ten shillings and Christie invited her home. One hot August afternoon in 1943, while Mrs Christie was away in Sheffield, she called again at 10 Rillington Place.

Christie held back from sex on this occasion, but Fuerst encouraged him. Once intercourse was over, he strangled her. Christie said he felt a great sense of peace after he had murdered her and was fascinated by the beauty of her corpse. He wanted to keep her, but his wife returned home unexpectedly and he had to bury her in the back garden that night. This had to be done stealthily as the communal lavatory was out there.

Despite this, Christie compared his first murder to an artist's first painting. 'It was thrilling because I had embarked on the career I had chosen for myself, the career of murder. But it was only the beginning,' he said later.

Christie quit the police force at the end of 1943. He went to work at the Ultra Radio Works in west London, where he met Muriel Eady. She suffered from catarrh and he said he had a remedy. One afternoon in October 1944, she came round to 10 Rillington Place and he showed her what he said was a patent inhaler. In fact, it was nothing more than a jar with perfumed water in it. There were two holes in the lid with rubber tubes attached. Unbeknownst to Muriel, one of them was connected to the gas pipe.

Christie persuaded her to inhale through the other tube, confident that the perfume would cover the smell of gas. As she lapsed into unconsciousness, he had sex with her, then strangled her. Christie was delighted at the thought that his second murder was so much cleverer than his first. All his careful planning had paid off. She, too, was buried in the garden. It was an area less than 20ft sq.

At Easter 1948, Timothy and Beryl Evans moved into the top-floor flat at 10 Rillington Place. Evans had been born in Merthyr Vale on 20 November 1924. He never knew his father, who had walked out of the house one day and was never seen or heard of again. Timothy Evans was educationally backward and had a speech impediment. In his early years, he could not pronounce his own name. His schooling was further held back by a foot injury which led to long spells in hospital.

Some years after her husband's disappearance, Timothy's mother obtained a certificate saying that he was presumed dead. In 1929, she married again and, during the Depression, the family moved to Notting Hill where, in 1947, Timothy married a local girl, Beryl Thorley.

Evans, then 24, had seen the 'To Let' sign outside 10 Rillington Place while living with his mother and step-father. Beryl was pregnant and the couple needed a place desperately, so they took the cramped attic flat.

On the floor below lived railwayman Charles Kitchener. He kept himself to himself; his eyesight was failing and he was often away in hospital. The ground floor was occupied by John and Ethel Christie.

The Evanses and the Christies got on well. Ethel was fond of the baby and looked after Geraldine when Beryl went to her part-time job.

In the summer of 1949, Beryl fell pregnant again. There was little money coming in and they were behind on the hire-purchase payments. Beryl wanted an abortion. Timothy, a Roman Catholic, forbade it. But Beryl was just 19 and did not want to be tied to a home and family. She was adamant and found that there was a back-street abortionist in the Edgware Road who would do the job for £1.

When Christie heard of her plans, he told Beryl that he could help her out. He could perform an abortion on her in the house. Later, he approached Timothy Evans, who said that he had not realised Christie knew anything about medical procedures. To convince him, Christie offered to show him one of his medical books. It was the first-aid manual of the St John Ambulance Brigade. Evans, who was barely literate, knew no better. He was impressed by the pictures.

On 8 November 1949, or the day before, Evans came home to find Christie waiting for him with bad news. The operation had not been a success, Christie said. Beryl had died.

Christie begged Evans not to go to the police. He would be charged with manslaughter as Beryl had died during an illegal abortion. Evans wanted his mother to look after the baby, but Christie said he would find someone to look after the child. When Evans returned from work on 10 November, Christie said that Geraldine had been taken to a couple in East Acton who would look after her.

Christie helped Evans sell off his furniture. With £40 in his pocket, Evans headed off back to Wales. But he could not get the fate of his young wife out of his mind. As a Catholic, he should have prevented her going through with the abortion. If he had, she would still be alive. Tormented with guilt, he walked into Merthyr Vale police station and confessed.

At first, Evans thought he could take the blame without implicating his friend Christie. Evans told the police that he had been given a bottle containing something that would cause a miscarriage by a man he met in a transport café. Although he did not mean to give it to his wife, she found it when he went out to work. When he returned, she was dead. He opened a drain outside the front door and dropped his wife's body down it.

The Merthyr Vale police contacted the station at Notting Hill. They sent officers to 10 Rillington Place. It took three of them to lift the manhole cover. The drain was empty. Back in Merthyr, Evans's statement was challenged. A detective told him he could not possibly have lifted the manhole cover himself. Evans made a second statement, this time implicating Christie. He said that Christie had performed an illegal abortion on his wife. She had died and, together, they had disposed of the body.

Police searched Rillington Place, but not very meticulously. They did not even notice the thighbone of Muriel Eady propped against the garden fence. But what police did find was a stolen briefcase, and Evans was arrested.

Christie went to the police station and made a statement about the Evans's domestic quarrels. Beryl, he said, had complained of her husband grabbing her by the throat. The police believed him. After all, Christie was a former policeman himself.

The house in Rillington Place was searched again. This time, the police found the body of Beryl Evans wrapped in a green tablecloth behind a stack of wood outside the wash-house; the body of baby Geraldine was found behind the door. Both had been strangled. Beryl's right eye and upper lip were swollen and there was bruising to her vagina. To the police, this confirmed it was a simple 'domestic'.

Evans was brought back to London. He made a statement saying he had strangled Beryl with a rope and put her in the outside wash-house after the Christies had gone to bed. Two days later, he had strangled the baby and put her body in the outhouse.

He was charged with the murder of both his wife and his daughter, but the Crown only proceeded with the murder of the baby. There could be no excuse for such a crime.

The trial took place at the Old Bailey in January 1950. In the witness box, Christie denied taking part in the abortion and said that he had been ill in bed on the day of Beryl's death. He apologised to the judge for speaking softly, but he said this was because he had been gassed in the First World War. The court was also told of his service as a Special Constable, giving the impression that he was a solid citizen and that his word was not to be doubted.

Evans gave his evidence poorly. His allegation that Beryl

died during an illegal abortion performed by Christie held no water as she had been strangled. And he had no possible explanation for the death of the baby. The jury was out for only 40 minutes. The verdict was guilty; the sentence – death by hanging.

To the end, Evans maintained that Christie had killed both Beryl and Geraldine and there was some public disquiet about the verdict. A petition with 18,000 signatures was sent to the Home Secretary, but he would not grant a reprieve and Evans was hanged on 9 March 1950.

Christie had got away with it. But on 14 December 1952, Christie said he was awakened by his wife Ethel going into convulsions. By now, she was elderly and arthritic. Christie decided it would be a kindness to put her out of her misery and strangled her.

For two days he kept his wife's body in the bed, then he pulled up the floorboards of the front room and buried her under them. He claimed that her loss caused him pain. They had been married for 32 years.

For the next four months, Christie went on a sex and murder spree. Kathleen Maloney was lured into his flat to pose for nude photographs. Her body was shoved in an alcove in the kitchen. Rita Nelson had just found out that she was pregnant when she visited 10 Rillington Place on 12 January 1953. She did not leave alive.

Christie had more trouble with Hectorina MacLennan, his final victim. He met her in a café and offered her a place to stay. But he was surprised when she turned up with her boyfriend. They stayed at Rillington Place together for three nights. On 6 March, Christie followed them to the Labour Exchange. While her boyfriend was signing on, Christie persuaded Hectorina to come back to the flat.

Christie had given her a drink and offered her a whiff of his inhaler. She did not like it. There was a struggle and he strangled her; then he had sex with her after she was dead. He bundled her body in the alcove with Kathleen Maloney, propping her in a sitting position with her bra hooked to Maloney's leg. Soon after, he moved out.

Once Beresford Brown had found the bodies in the alcove and others had been found under the floorboards and buried in the back garden, the hunt was on.

The day he left 10 Rillington Place, Christie had booked into Rowton House, (now the Mount Pleasant Hotel), in King's Cross Road for seven nights. But he soon moved on, wandering uneasily back and forth across London. There were numerous reported sightings of Christie; few were genuine. On 19 March 1953, at around 11.00pm, the chief crime reporter of the *News of the World*, Norman Rae, received a phone call.

'Do you recognize my voice?' the caller asked.

Rae did. He had met Christie before, in 1950, during the murder trial of Timothy Evans.

'I can't stand any more,' Christie said. 'They're hunting me like a dog.'

In return for a meal, a smoke and a warm place to sit, he said would give the *News of the World* an exclusive. Rae warned him that, afterwards, he would have to call the police. Christie agreed and they arranged to meet at 1.30am, outside Wood Green Town Hall.

Rae parked outside the Town Hall, away from the street lamps, opened the car door and waited. Christie approached. Then, purely by chance, two policemen on their beat happened by. Thinking he had been betrayed, Christie ran off.

Two days later, PC Thomas Ledger saw a man leaning over the embankment near Putney Bridge, possibly contemplating suicide. When Constable Ledger approached him, he said he was John Waddington of 35 Westbourne Grove. But the young officer recognised him and asked him to turn out his pockets. One contained a 1950 newspaper cutting of Timothy Evans's murder trial. The hunt for Christie was over.

Christie made detailed confessions and provided a variety of explanations for the killings – the prostitutes had forced themselves upon him and things had got out of hand; his wife had had to be put out of her misery; Muriel Eady and Beryl Evans had also been mercy killings.

At his trial, Christie pleaded not guilty by virtue of insanity. But he could not disguise the fact that he had extensively planned the killing of his victims; he had constructed a special apparatus to gas four of them.

The jury found Christie guilty and the judge sentenced him to death. There was no appeal. The only problem the law had was the conviction of Timothy Evans for the murder of his wife Beryl – a murder to which Christie had now confessed. A formal inquiry was set up, which found that two murderers had been operating in 10 Rillington Place – and that Christie had told the truth at Evans's trial but had lied at his own. Christie was hanged at Pentonville Prison at 9.00am on 15 July 1953.

Evans was given a posthumous pardon in 1966 and his remains were moved from Pentonville Prison and reburied in St Patrick's Roman Catholic Cemetery in Leytonstone. In 2003, his sister and half-sister were given *ex gratia* payments in compensation for the miscarriage of justice.

3

BONFIRES AND BEASTIES

Dennis Nilsen was famous for 'killing for company' – which was also the title of a book about him by Brian Masters. He would keep the body of his victims in his flat until the smell of decomposition grew too much for him. He was eventually caught because he cooked up their flesh and flushed the remains down the lavatory, blocking the drains.

But that is not the whole story. Nilsen disposed of his first 12 victims by scattering their organs in the back garden for what he called the 'wee beasties of the night' to eat; the remains of others were burned on bonfires and the bones buried. In the garden of his flat in Melrose Avenue, north London, numerous fragments of bone were found. Of the twelve men he killed there, eight have never been identified.

Nilsen was born in Fraserburgh, a small town on the

bleak north-east coast of Scotland, on 23 November 1945. His father was a Norwegian soldier who had escaped to Scotland after the German invasion of his homeland in 1940. He had married Betty Whyte, a local girl, in 1942. The marriage did not work out and Betty continued to live with her parents. A few years later, the Nilsens were divorced.

Dennis grew up with his mother, elder brother and younger sister, but the strongest influences on his young life were his stern and pious grandparents. Their Christian faith was so strict that they banned alcohol from the house, and the radio and the cinema were considered instruments of the Devil. Nilsen's grandmother would not even cook on the Lord's day and their Sunday dinner had to be prepared on Saturday.

As a boy, Dennis Nilsen was sullen and intensely withdrawn. The only person who could penetrate his private world was his grandfather, Andrew Whyte. A fisherman, he was Nilsen's hero. He would regale the little boy with tales of the sea and his ancestors lost beneath its churning waves.

When Andrew Whyte died of a heart attack at sea in 1951, he was brought home and laid out on the dining-room table. Dennis was invited to come and see his grandad's body. At the age of six, he got his first glimpse of a corpse. From that moment, the images of death and love fused in his mind.

He left school at 15 and joined the Army. After basic training, he was sent to the catering corps. There he was taught how to sharpen knives – and how to dissect a carcass. During his life in the Army, Nilsen only had one close friend, whom he would persuade to pose for photographs, sprawled on the ground as if he had just been killed in battle.

One night in Aden, Nilsen was drunk and fell asleep in the back of a cab. When he awoke, he found himself naked, locked in the boot. When the Arab cab driver returned, Nilsen played dead. Then, as the driver manhandled him out of the boot, Nilsen grabbed a car jack and beat him around the head. Nilsen never knew whether he had killed the man or not, but the incident had a profound effect on him.

'The next morning I was full of horror at what had happened to me,' he said. 'I had nightmares afterwards of being raped, tortured and mutilated.'

After 11 years in the Army, Nilsen left and joined the police force. His training included a mortuary visit, where recently qualified constables were initiated in the gruesome habit of viewing the dead. But Nilsen was not repelled. He found the partially dissected corpses fascinating.

Nilsen did well in the police, but his private life was gradually disintegrating. Death became an obsession. He would pretend to be a corpse himself, masturbating in front of a mirror with blue paint smeared on his lips and his skin whitened with talcum powder.

Since his teens, he had been aware of his attraction towards other men, but in the Army and in the police force he had somehow managed to repress it. Then, 11 months after he had joined the police, he was on the beat when he caught two men committing an act of gross indecency in a parked car. Aware of his own inclinations, he could not bring himself to arrest them and he decided to resign.

He went to work interviewing applicants at the Jobcentre in London's Charing Cross Road. There he became branch secretary of the civil service union and developed increasingly radical political views. Nevertheless, his work was good enough to earn him promotion to executive officer at the Jobcentre in Kentish Town, north London.

Despite his professional progress, Nilsen was lonely. In 1975, he met a young man called David Gallichen outside a pub. They moved into a flat at 195 Melrose Avenue together, with a cat and a dog called Bleep. Gallichen, or 'Twinkle' as Nilsen called him, stayed at home and decorated the flat while Nilsen went to work. They made home movies together and spent a lot of time drinking and talking. Gallichen moved out in 1977 and Nilsen was plunged back into a life of loneliness.

On New Year's Eve 1978, Nilsen met a teenage Irish boy in a pub and invited him back to Melrose Avenue. They were too drunk to have sex. When Nilsen woke in the morning, the boy was lying fast asleep beside him. He was afraid that when the boy woke up he would leave – and Nilsen wanted him to stay. Their clothes were thrown together in a heap on the floor. Nilsen leant over and grabbed his tie, which he then put around the boy's neck and pulled. The boy woke immediately and began to struggle. They rolled on to the floor, but Nilsen kept pulling on the tie.

After about a minute, the boy's body went limp but he was still breathing. Nilsen went to the kitchen and filled a bucket with water. He brought the bucket back and held the boy's head underwater until he drowned. Now he had to stay.

Nilsen carried the dead boy into the bathroom and gave him a bath. He dried the corpse lovingly, then dressed it in clean socks and underpants. For a while, he just lay in bed holding the dead boy, then he put him on the floor and he went to sleep.

The following day, he planned to hide the body under the floor, but rigor mortis had stiffened the joints, making the corpse hard to handle. So he left the body out while he went to work. When the corpse had loosened up, Nilsen undressed it again and washed it. This time he masturbated beside it and found he could not stop playing with it and admiring it.

The Killer expected to be arrested at any moment, even while he played with the corpse. But no one came. It seemed no one had missed the dead boy. After a week living happily with the corpse, Nilsen hid it under the floorboards. Seven months later, he cut the body up and burnt it in the back garden. The victim was later identified as 14-year-old Stephen Dean Holmes.

Nilsen's first experience of murder frightened him. He was determined it would not happen again and decided to give up drinking. But Nilsen was lonely; he liked to go to pubs to meet people and talk to them. Soon he slipped off the wagon.

Nearly a year later, on 3 December 1979, Nilsen met Kenneth Ockenden, a Canadian tourist, in a pub in Soho. Nilsen had taken leave from work that afternoon and took Ockenden on a sightseeing tour of London. Ockenden agreed to go back to Nilsen's flat for something to eat. After a visit to the off-licence, they sat in front of the television eating ham, eggs and chips and drinking beer, whisky and rum.

As the evening wore on, disturbing feelings began to grow inside Nilsen. He liked Ockenden, but realised that he would soon be leaving and going back to Canada. A feeling of desolation crept over him. It was the same feeling he had had when he killed the Irish boy.

Late that night, when they were both very drunk, Ockenden was listening to music through earphones. Nilsen put the flex of the earphones around Ockenden's neck and dragged him struggling across the floor. When he was dead, Nilsen took the earphones off and put them on himself. He poured himself another drink and listened to records.

In the early hours, he stripped the corpse and carried it over his shoulder into the bathroom, where he washed it. When the body was clean and dry, he put it on the bed and went to sleep next to it.

In the morning, he put the body in a cupboard and went to work. That evening, he took the body out and dressed it in clean socks, underpants and vest. He took some photographs of it, then lay it next to him on the bed. For the next two weeks, Nilsen would watch TV in the evening with Ockenden's body propped up in an armchair next to him. Last thing at night, he would undress it, wrap it in some curtains and place the body under the floorboards.

As Ockenden had gone missing from a hotel, his disappearance made the news for a few days. Again, Nilsen was convinced that he was about to be arrested at any moment. Several people in the pub, on the bus, at the sights they had visited and even in the local off-licence had seen them together. But still there was no knock on the door. From then on, Nilsen felt that he could pursue his murderous hobby unfettered.

Although plenty of people visited the flat in Melrose Avenue and emerged alive, Nilsen now began deliberately to seek out victims. He would go to pubs where lonely young homosexuals hung out. He would buy them drinks, offer advice and invite them back to his flat for something to eat. Many accepted.

One of them was Martin Duffey. After a disturbed childhood, he ran away from home and ended up in London, sleeping in railway stations. He went back to Nilsen's flat and, after two cans of beer, crawled into bed. When he was asleep, Nilsen strangled him. While he was still barely alive, Nilsen dragged his unconscious body into the kitchen, filled the sink with water and held his head under for four minutes.

Nilsen then went through the standard procedure of stripping and bathing the corpse, then he took it to bed. He talked to it, complimenting Duffey on his body. He kissed it all over and masturbated over it. Nilsen kept the body in a cupboard for a few days. When it started to swell up, he put it under the floorboards.

In the summer of 1980, the bodies of Ockenden and Duffey were producing a smell that was hard to disguise. Nilsen decided that he must get rid of them. He lifted the floorboards and lifted out the putrefying corpses. Laying them on the kitchen floor, he cut them up and stuffed the pieces into bags. There were some old suitcases in the cupboard under the stairs. He put the bags in them and carried them out to the back garden. He put them in the garden shed that he had originally built for the dog, Bleep. He covered them with newspapers and bricks, after adding some deodorant sticks to the gruesome pile.

The next victim was 27-year-old Billy Sutherland. He died because he was a nuisance. Nilsen didn't fancy him but, after meeting him on a pub crawl, Sutherland followed him home. Nilsen vaguely remembered strangling him. There was certainly a dead body in the flat in the morning.

Nilsen did not even know some of his victims by name. He was not much interested in them, only their bodies – their dead bodies. The murder routine was always much the same, that part was mechanical. But once they were dead, they really turned him on. Touching the corpse would give him an erection.

In fact Nilsen would never think of his victims' bodies lying around his flat while he was out at work. But in the evening when he got home, he could not help playing with them. He was thrilled to own their beautiful bodies and was fascinated by the mystery of death. He would hold the corpse in a passionate embrace and talk to it and, when he was finished with it, he would stuff it back under the floorboards.

By the end of 1980, he had six more corpses of identified victims on his hands, along with the body parts in the garden shed. Three were under the floorboards; others were decapitated and the heads and torsos were shoved in suitcases. One would not fit, so he cut off the arms and hands, and left them under a bush outside the French windows. The arms and hands lay there for over a year.

With flies buzzing around the house, it reached the point when Nilsen decided that he had to get rid of some of the remains. The procedure was grisly. First, he prised up the floorboards and uncovered the body. Then he took it by the ankles, pulled it up through the gap in the floor and along the ground into the kitchen onto a piece of plastic sheeting.

Before he began, he had to knock back a Bacardi and Coke, then masturbate beside the body. It was, he said, his way of saying goodbye. He stripped naked to avoid soiling his clothes. Then he prepared a small bowl of water, a kitchen knife, some paper tissues and plastic bags. He needed a couple more drinks before he could start. He removed the vest and underpants from the body. With the knife, he cut off the head. There was very little blood. He put the head in the kitchen sink, washed it and put it in a carrier bag. He then cut off the hands, then the feet. He washed them in the sink and dried them, wrapping each one in paper towelling and put them in plastic carrier bags.

He cut the corpses from the navel to the breastbone and removed the intestines, stomach, kidneys and liver. From there, he would break through the diaphragm and remove the heart and lungs. He put all these organs into a plastic carrier bag.

Then he cut the remains in two, separating the top half of the body from the bottom half. He removed the arms and then the legs below the knee, putting the parts in black carrier bags. The chest and ribcage went into a large bag; the thighs, buttocks and private parts – still in one piece – in another. These packages went back under the floorboards, although he would leave the bag containing the entrails and organs out.

Every so often, he stopped to be sick in the sink. There was a cooling breeze from the French windows, but he would not walk over to them, because he wanted to avoid treading on the body parts that were spread around the living room.

After the first body had been dissected, he uncovered the next body which had been there longer. Again, he pulled it out by the ankles and into the kitchen. There were maggots on the surface of the skin. He poured salt on these and brushed them off. The corpse was discoloured. He was violently sick and steadied himself with a few more glasses of spirits before repeating the process of dissection. Everything was done with a kitchen knife; he had no saws or power tools.

When the task was complete, he replaced the packages under the floorboards and had a bath. Afterwards, he would listen to music on the headphones and get really drunk, then take the dog out for a walk in Gladstone Park.

'Bleep always got a bit apprehensive and stayed in the garden while I carried out these tasks,' said Nilsen.

While removing the internal organs was the messiest part of the procedure – it involved vile fluids and stomach-churning smells – these were the easiest to dispose of. He dumped them between the double fence at the side of the garden for rats, birds and insects to feast upon.

He had two bonfires in the back garden at Melrose Avenue for burning body parts. When that caused no complaint, one cold day at the beginning of December 1980, he built a huge bonfire on the wasteland just beyond the garden fence, pulling off a couple of palings to gain access. Early the following morning, he pulled up the floorboards again, wrapped the body parts in carpets and dragged them across the garden to the bonfire. He pushed them deep under the timber and some discarded furniture he had collected.

The garden shed was close to the gap in the fence and the door obscured the view from the house. Nilsen then started shifting the body parts he had stored there. The suitcases on top were still intact and he pushed them through the gap in the fence. Those at the bottom of the pile were crushed and rotten. As he moved them, they split apart, spilling decomposing flesh and bone along the path.

The heads were now unrecognisable. He shoved them

into the middle of the bonfire. Once everything was hidden from sight, he began cleaning up the shed, which was full of maggots and flies. Then he stuffed newspapers and magazines around the fire, sprinkled them with lighter fuel and set light to it. He chucked an old car tyre on top to disguise the smell of burning flesh.

All day, Nilsen kept an eye on the fire, throwing more wood on to it when necessary. The fire attracted local kids who wanted to dance around it. He warned them to keep back.

Nilsen was mesmerised by the flames. He could not believe what he had done and now thought that he might awake from a bad dream or, at least, be able to forget about what had happened for ever.

As the flames died down, a charred skull appeared in the middle of the cinders. Nilsen crushed it with a rake. Once everything had been reduced to ashes, he covered them over with bricks from the shed. After he had bathed and dressed, he took the Tube to the West End, where he picked up a young man and took him back to Melrose Avenue in a taxi. In the morning, he walked him to Willesden Underground station and Nilsen began to believe that his days of killing for company were behind him.

But his killing spree was far from over. Within a month, he had picked up his eighth victim in the West End after the pubs closed and took him home. This person's dissected remains went under the floorboards. He was soon joined by three more. By August, there were four bodies under the floorboards and the smell was overpowering even though he was spraying disinfectant around every day.

One Friday, he decided that he must do something about the problem, as he later explained in detail to the police:

I sat and deliberated this task reluctantly. I fortified myself with about half a bottle of drink before lifting up the floorboards. I removed the intact bundles one at a time, placed them on the kitchen stone floor and unwrapped the bundles one at a time. I put the wrapping to one side. I removed the clothing from the bodies and set about dissecting them. The smell was grossly unpleasant and, in some cases, there existed large colonies of maggots. I dissected the bodies and wrapped the parts in white kitchen towel, rolls of which I had an adequate supply. I tightly re-wrapped the parts in smaller compact bundles and put them to one side. I treated the three bodies in this fashion until all was complete and a number of bundles lay on the kitchen floor. I re-packed the bundles in the space under the floorboards, packed them with earth and deodorant tablets.

Again, the internal organs had been put in separate bags and had not been returned under the floorboards. As before, these were taken out into the back garden and dumped in the gap between the two fences where they would be eaten by scavenging animals.

Some of his murders were terrifyingly casual. Nilsen found his 12th victim, 24-year-old Malcolm Barlow, collapsed on the pavement in Melrose Avenue. Barlow was an epileptic and said that the pills he was taking made his legs give way. Nilsen carried him home and called an ambulance. When he was released from hospital the next day, Barlow returned to the Melrose Avenue flat where Nilsen prepared a meal. Barlow began drinking, even though Nilsen warned him not to mix alcohol with the new pills he had been prescribed. When Barlow collapsed, Nilsen could not be bothered to call an ambulance again and strangled him, then carried on drinking until bedtime. The space under the floorboards was already full of dismembered corpses, so the following morning Nilsen stuffed Barlow's body in the cupboard under the sink. Now that he had completely run out of storage space, Nilsen decided it was time to move. But he could hardly leave the bodies behind. He told the police:

I made a huge, well-constructed bonfire using furnishings, cabinets and things from the house, and left a sizable hollow at the centre of the structure. This I did the day before. Early in the morning, I lifted the floorboards and started to pack the packages into the centre of the wooden structure, the base of which was two large doors on house bricks. I did not replace the floorboards this time. Going to the kitchen, I opened the doors of the cupboard under the kitchen sink. I noticed that the body had become bloated. I removed the body and dragged it through the house and laid it inside the structure. I covered the entire structure with more wooden posts and palings, and all the bundles of paper from under the floorboards were pushed aside. The opening was sealed with more wood and the bonfire set alight. It was positioned about 15ft from a point exactly halfway between the French window and the kitchen window. The fire started early morning. There were spurts, bangs, cracks and hisses, a continual hissing and sizzling coming from the fire. This was what I took to be fat and other parts of the bodies burning.

He threw other rubbish from the flat on to the fire. When another resident came to see what was going on, Nilsen explained that he was moving out the next day and was burning the waste he could not take with him.

Before he left, he checked under the floorboards to make sure that he had not left any body parts behind. It was dark and he could only see one or two bits of clothing. Then he nailed the floorboards back in position. After a quick check around the flat to see if he had left anything unaccounted for, he went out into the garden. First, he checked the shed; then he checked the ashes of the latest fire.

'Some of it looked like bone splinters or even small pieces of skull, probably not identifiable as skull to the casual observer,' he said.

He took the garden roller and ran it over the ashes several times, crushing the remaining bone fragments. It was then that he remembered the arm and hand under the bush outside the French windows. He broke up the large bones with a shovel and flung them over the garden fence. A local dog was seen chomping on one some time later. The hole under the bush was then filled with ashes.

Nilsen moved to a small attic flat at 23 Cranley Gardens. This was a deliberate attempt to stop his murderous career. He could not kill people, he thought, if he had no floorboards to hide them under and no garden to burn them in.

He had several casual encounters at his new flat, picking men up at night and letting them go in the morning, unmolested. This made him elated. Again, he thought he had finally broken the cycle.

But then John Howlett, or 'Guardsman John' as Nilsen called him, came back to Cranley Gardens with him and Nilsen could not help himself. He strangled Howlett with a strap and drowned him. A few days later, he strangled another man, Graham Allen, while he was eating an omelette.

The death of his final victim, Stephen Sinclair, upset Nilsen. Sinclair was a drifter and a drug addict. When they met, Nilsen felt sorry for him and bought him a hamburger. Back at Cranley Gardens, he slumped in a chair in a stupor and Nilsen decided to relieve him of the pain of his miserable life. He got a piece of string from the kitchen, but it was not long enough. Then he got his one and only remaining tie and choked the life out of his unconscious victim.

Killing in Cranley Gardens presented Nilsen with a problem. He was forced to dispose of the bodies by dissecting them, boiling the flesh from the bones, dicing up the remains and flushing them down the toilet. Unfortunately, the sewage system in Muswell Hill was not built to handle dissected corpses.

The drains at 23 Cranley Gardens had been blocked for five days when, on 8 February 1983, Dyno-Rod sent Michael Cattran to investigate. He quickly determined that the problem was not inside, but outside the house. At the side of the house, he found the manhole that led to the sewers. He removed the cover and climbed in.

BONFIRES AND BEASTIES

At the bottom of the access shaft, he found a glutinous grey sludge. The smell was awful. As he examined it, more sludge came out of the pipe that led from the house. He called his manager and told him that he thought the substance he had found was human flesh.

Next morning, Cattran and his boss returned to the manhole, but the sludge had disappeared. No amount of rainfall could have flushed it through. Someone had been down there and removed it.

Cattran put his hand inside the pipe that connected to the house and pulled out some more meat and four small bones. One of the tenants in the house said that they had heard footsteps on the stairs in the night and suspected that the man who lived in the attic flat had been down to the manhole. They called the police.

Detective Chief Inspector Peter Jay took the flesh and bones to Charing Cross Hospital. A pathologist there confirmed that the flesh was, indeed, human.

The tenant of the attic flat was out at work when DCI Jay got back to Cranley Gardens. At 5.40pm that day, Nilsen returned. Inspector Jay met him at the front door and introduced himself. He said he had come about the drains. Nilsen remarked that it was odd that the police should be interested in drains. When Nilsen let him into the flat, Jay said that the drains contained human remains.

'Good grief! How awful!' Nilsen exclaimed.

Jay told him to stop messing about. 'Where's the rest of the body?' he asked.

After a short pause, Nilsen said, 'In two plastic bags in the wardrobe next door. I'll show you.'

He showed DCI Jay the wardrobe. The smell coming from it confirmed his story.

'I'll tell you everything,' Nilsen said. 'I want to get it off my chest ... not here, but at the police station.'

The police could scarcely believe their ears when Nilsen admitted killing 15 or 16 men. In the wardrobe in Nilsen's flat, the police found two large, black bin-liners. In one, they found a shopping bag containing the left side of a man's chest, including the arm. A second bag contained the right side of a chest and arm; in a third, there was a torso with no arms, legs or head; a fourth was full of human offal. The unbearable stench indicated that the bags had evidently been closed for some time and the contents had rotted.

In the second bin-liner, there were two heads – one with the flesh boiled away, the other largely intact – and another torso. The arms were still attached, but the hands were missing. One of the heads belonged to Stephen Sinclair. Nilsen had severed it only four days earlier and had started simmering it in a pot on the kitchen stove.

Under a drawer in the bathroom, the police found Sinclair's pelvis and legs. In a tea chest in Nilsen's bedroom, there was another torso, a skull and more bones.

The police also examined the back garden at 195 Melrose Avenue. A large forensics team had to be brought in. They found human ash and over 1,000 fragments of bone, enough to determine that at least eight people, probably more, had been cremated there.

Nilsen was eventually charged with six counts of murder and three of attempted murder. His solicitor had one simple question for Nilsen: 'Why?'

'I'm hoping you will tell me that,' Nilsen said.

Nilsen pleaded not guilty on the basis of 'diminished responsibility'.

One of the most extraordinary witnesses at the trial was Carl Stottor. Nilsen had tried to strangle him three times, but somehow his frail body had clung to life. Nilsen had then dragged him to the bath and held him underwater. Somehow, Stottor had found the strength to push himself up three times and beg for mercy. But Nilsen pushed him down again. Thinking he was dead, Nilsen took Stottor's body back into the bedroom and smoked a cigarette. Then Bleep, Nilsen's dog, began to lick Stottor's face and the young man began to revive. Nilsen could easily have snuffed out his life then and there. Instead, he rubbed Stottor's legs to stimulate his circulation. He wrapped him with blankets and nursed him back to life. When he had recovered sufficiently, Nilsen walked him to the Tube station and wished him luck.

Nilsen had left another survivor to testify against him. Paul Nobbs had slept at Cranley Gardens one night and woke at 2.00am with a splitting headache. When he woke again in the morning, he found red marks around his neck. Nilsen advised him to see a doctor. At the hospital, Nobbs was told that he had been half strangled. He assumed that his attacker had been Nilsen, but did not report the assault to the police, perhaps fearing they would dismiss the attack as a domestic squabble.

BODIES IN THE BACK GARDEN

In November 1983, Nilsen was convicted of the attempted murder of Stottor and Nobbs, plus the actual murder of six others. He was sentenced to life imprison-ment with the recommendation that he serve at least 25 years, although he will probably never be released.

Nilsen said he did not lose sleep over what he has done, or have nightmares about it. Nor does he have any tears for his victims or their relatives.

4

BACKYARD CANNIBAL

Like Dennis Nilsen, Milwaukee mass murderer Jeffrey Dahmer kept the corpses of his victims around his home. But he wanted to possess them even more completely, so he ended up eating their flesh. That way they would be a part of him and stay with him forever. When he was finally arrested after a murderous career of 13 years, he was found to have a fridge full of human body parts. However, when he was a kid in rural Ohio, he disposed of his first victim in the backyard.

Dahmer began his killing spree in 1978 when he was 18. At that time, he was living in Bath, Ohio, and his parents were going through an acrimonious divorce. Dahmer's father had already left and his mother was away on a vacation. Dahmer was alone in the house and feeling very neglected. So he went out looking for company. He picked up a hitch-hiker, a 19-year-old white youth named Steven

Hicks who had spent the day at a rock concert. They got on well and Dahmer took Hicks back to his parents' house at 4480 West Bath Road. They had a few beers and talked about their lives. Then Hicks said that he had to go. Dahmer begged him to stay, but Hicks was insistent. So Dahmer made him stay. He picked up a heavy dumbbell, beat him around the head and strangled him.

Then he stripped his victim's body and caressed and fondled it, then masturbated over it. Afterwards, the full horror of what he had done swept over him. 'I was out of my mind with fear that night,' he later told psychiatrist Dr Kenneth Smail. 'I did not know what to do. I had gone to such an extreme.'

When darkness fell, Dahmer dragged Hicks's body into the crawl space under the house and dismembered it with a hunting knife. He had had plenty of practice. His childhood hobby had been dissecting animals. While the blood soaked into the earth, he wrapped Hicks's body parts in plastic bags and stashed them there. But the stench of rotting flesh soon permeated the house.

Dahmer spent the whole of the next day wondering what to do. He decided that he should dump the remains in a ravine ten miles away. After a few beers, he loaded them into his car and set off. On the way, he was tailed by a police car that eventually signalled him to stop. It was 3.00am and Dahmer had been driving on the left-hand side of the road.

When a backup arrived, Dahmer was ordered to get out of the car. This was before the introduction of the breathalyzer, so he was told to put his finger on the end of his nose and to walk in a straight line. He passed both tests.

With a flashlight, one of the cops spotted the garbage bags on the back seat of his car. 'What's that smell?' he was asked. Dahmer said that it was trash he was taking to the garbage dump. Why so late? Dahmer explained that his parents were getting a divorce and he could not sleep. He thought a drive might clear his mind. The cop gave him a ticket for erratic driving.

Thirteen years later, the officer who had stopped him, Patrolman Richard Munsey, had become Lieutenant Munsey and he was sent by the Ohio Police Department to Milwaukee to interview Dahmer. It was only then that he discovered the mistake he had made that night when he was a rookie cop.

Returning home, Dahmer put the remains back in the crawl space. Then he opened the bags to find the head. He carried it up to his bedroom, put it on the floor and masturbated over it.

That following night, Dahmer took the remains and buried them in a nearby wood. But later he became afraid that local children would discover the grave. He had played there as a kid, digging up bones and flints; other kids might do the same. So he dug up the body parts, stripped the flesh and dissolved it in acid. The resultant brown sludge was flushed down a drainpipe.

Then he pulverised the bones with a sledgehammer until there were no bone fragments larger than a small person's hand. Then he scattered the pieces around his garden and the neighbouring property. In the backyard, he also burnt Hicks's clothes and wallet and anything that might identify the victim. Then he took the necklace Hicks had been wearing when he picked him up and the knife he had used to cut him to pieces and tossed them off a bridge into the Cuyahoga River. It was ten years before Dahmer killed again ... but he already knew he was doomed.

'That night in Ohio,' he said, 'that one impulsive night ... nothing's been normal since then. It taints your whole life. After it happened, I thought that I would just try to live as normally as possible and bury it, but things like that don't stay buried. I didn't think it would, but it does, it taints your whole life.'

In 1986, Dahmer, then aged 26, was sentenced to a year's probation for exposing himself and masturbating publicly in front of two 12-year-old boys. He claimed he was urinating and promised the judge that it would not happen again.

By then Dahmer had moved to Milwaukee to live with his grandmother. He was a loner. He would hang out in gay bars; if he did strike up a conversation with another customer, he would slip drugs into their drink. Often they would end up in a coma. Dahmer made no attempt to rape them or kill them, he was simply experimenting. But when the owner of the Club Bar ended up unconscious in hospital, Dahmer was barred.

Six days after the end of his probation, he picked up 24-year-old Stephen Tuomi in a gay club. They went to the Ambassador Hotel to have sex. When Dahmer awoke, he found Tuomi lying dead next to him; there was blood around his mouth and bruising on his neck.

Dahmer had been drunk the night before and realised that he must have strangled Tuomi. Now he was alone in a hotel room with a corpse and any minute the porter would be checking whether the room had been vacated. He rushed out and bought a large suitcase. He stuffed Tuomi's body into it and took a taxi back to his grandmother's house. The taxi-driver even helped him drag the heavy case inside. Dahmer then cut up the body and put the bits into plastic bags which he put out for the garbage truck. He performed this task so well that he left no traces at all. When the police called round to ask him about the disappearance of Tuomi, there was no sign of a body and Dahmer found that he had got away with his second murder.

Sex, companionship and death were now inextricably linked in Dahmer's mind. Four months later, he picked up a young male prostitute. They went back to Dahmer's grandmother's house to have sex in the basement. Dahmer gave the boy a drink laced with a powerful sedative. When the young man was unconscious, he strangled him. He dismembered the corpse, stripped off the flesh, pulverised the bones and scattered the pieces. No remains were ever found.

Two months later, Dahmer met 14-year-old Native American male prostitute James Doxator who was broke. Dahmer offered him money to perform in a video. He had oral sex with Dahmer, in his grandmother's basement.

When it was over, Dahmer offered him a drink, drugged him, strangled him and disposed of the corpse.

In March 1988, Dahmer picked up 22-year-old bisexual Richard Guerrero and took him back to his grandmother's. He drugged him, strangled him and performed oral sex on the corpse. Dahmer put the body out with the trash, but kept the skull for a couple of months.

Dahmer's grandmother began to complain of the smell that persisted even after the rubbish had been collected. She then found a patch of blood in the garage. Dahmer said that he had been skinning animals out there. She accepted this excuse, but made it clear that she wanted him to move out.

Then Dahmer found himself a small apartment in a run-down, predominantly black area. On his first night there, he lured Keison Sinthasomphone, a 13-year-old Laotian boy back to the flat and drugged him. The boy, whose older brother later perished at Dahmer's hands, somehow managed to escape. Dahmer was arrested and charged with sexual assault and enticing a minor for immoral purposes. He spent a week in jail, then was released on bail.

His father had already given up on him, saying his son 'would never be more than he seemed to be – a liar, an alcoholic, a thief, an exhibitionist, a molester of children. I could not imagine how he had become such a ruined soul ... For the first time, I no longer believed that my efforts and resources alone would be enough to save my son. There was something missing in Jeff ... we call it a "conscience" ... that had either died or had never been alive in the first place.'

But Dahmer could not contain his compulsion to kill. While out on bail, he picked up handsome 26-year-old black bisexual Anthony Sears. Fearing that the police were watching his apartment, he took Sears back to his grandmother's basement. They had sex, then Dahmer drugged him and dismembered his body. He disposed of Sears's corpse in the rubbish, but boiled the flesh off the head so he could keep the skull as a souvenir.

Back in court, the District Attorney pushed for five years' imprisonment for his assault on Keison Sinthasomphone. Dahmer's attorney argued that the attack was a one-off offence. His client was a homosexual and a heavy drinker, and needed psychiatric help, not punishment. Dahmer got five years' probation and a year on a correction programme.

It did not help. Dahmer was now set in his murderous ways. He picked up a young black stranger in a club and offered him money to pose for nude photographs. Back in Dahmer's flat, the youth accepted a drink. It was drugged. Once he was unconsciousness, Dahmer strangled him, stripped him and performed oral sex with the corpse. Then he dismembered the body, again keeping the skull, which he painted grey.

He picked up another notorious homosexual known as 'the Sheikh' and did the same to him – only this time he had oral sex before he drugged and strangled his victim.

The next victim, a 15-year-old Hispanic, was luckier. Dahmer offered him $200 to pose nude. He undressed but Dahmer neglected to drug him before attacking him with a rubber mallet. Dahmer tried to strangle him, but he fought back. Eventually, Dahmer calmed down. The boy promised not to inform the police and Dahmer let him go, even calling him a taxi.

The next day, when he went to hospital for treatment, the boy broke his promise and spoke to the police. But he begged them not to let his foster parents find out that he was a homosexual and the police dropped the matter altogether.

The next time Dahmer picked up a victim, a few weeks later, he craved more than his usual fare of sex, murder and grisly dismemberment. He decided to keep the skeleton and bleached it with acid. He dissolved most of the flesh in the acid, but kept the biceps intact in the fridge.

When neighbours began to complain of the smell of putrefying flesh coming from his flat, Dahmer apologised. He said that the fridge was broken and he was waiting to get it fixed.

Dahmer's next victim, 23-year-old David Thomas, was not gay. He had a girlfriend and a three-year-old daughter, but accepted Dahmer's offer to come back to his apartment for money. After drugging him, Dahmer realised that he did not really fancy his latest pickup anyway. But fearing that Thomas might make trouble when he woke up, he killed him. This time he took more pleasure in the dismemberment, photographing it step by step.

Seventeen-year-old aspiring model Curtis Straughter was engaged in oral sex with Dahmer when the sleeping potion took effect. Dahmer strangled him and, again, photographed the dismemberment. Once again, his skull was kept as a trophy.

Nineteen-year-old Errol Lindsey's murder proceeded along exactly the same lines. Dahmer offered him money to pose for nude photographs, then drugged, strangled and dismembered him. The grisly process was photographed and his skull was added to Dahmer's collection.

Thirty-one-year-old deaf mute, Tony Hughes, also accepted $50 to pose nude. But by this time, Dahmer had become so blasé about the whole procedure that he kept Hughes's body in his bedroom for several days before he cut it up.

Dahmer's next victim was Keison Sinthasomphone's older brother, 14-year-old Konerak. Again, things went badly wrong. Dahmer drugged the boy, stripped him and raped him but then, instead of strangling him, Dahmer went out to buy some beer. On his way back to the apartment, Dahmer saw Konerak out on the street. He was naked, bleeding and talking to two black girls. When Dahmer grabbed him, the girls hung on to him. One of them had called the police and two patrol cars arrived.

The police wanted to know what all the trouble was about; Dahmer said that he and Konerak had had a lover's tiff. He managed to convince them that 14-year-old Konerak was really 19 and, back at his apartment, he showed them Polaroids of Konerak in his underwear which seemed to back up his story that they were lovers. The police did not realise that the pictures had been taken earlier that day, while Konerak was drugged.

Throughout all this, Konerak sat passively on the sofa, thinking his ordeal was over. In fact, it had only just begun.

The police accepted Dahmer's story and left. Konerak was strangled immediately and then dismembered. The three policemen involved were later dismissed.

Dahmer attended Gay Pride Day in Chicago and, on the way back, picked up another would-be model, Matt Turner. Back at Dahmer's apartment, he was also strangled and dismembered.

When Dahmer picked up 23-year-old Jeremiah Weinberger in a gay club, Weinberger asked his former room-mate whether he should go with Dahmer. The room-mate said, 'Sure, he looks OK.'

Dahmer seems to have liked Weinberger. They spent the whole of the next day together having sex. Then Weinberger looked at the clock and said it was time to go – whereupon Dahmer said he should stay for just one more drink. His head ended up in the freezer, next to Matt Turner's.

When Dahmer lost his job, he knew only one thing would make him feel better. He picked up a 24-year-old black man called Oliver Lacy, took him back to his apartment, strangled him and sodomised his dead body.

Four days later, 25-year-old Joseph Bradeholt – who was married with two children – accepted Dahmer's offer of money for nude photographs and, according to Dahmer, willingly joined in oral sex with him. His dismembered torso was left to soak in a dustbin filled with acid.

By the time Dahmer had killed 17 men, all in much the same way, he was getting so casual that it was inevitable that he would get caught. On 22 June 1991, he met Tracy Edwards, a young black man who had just arrived from

Mississippi. He was with a number of friends. Dahmer invited them all back to his apartment for a party. He and Edwards would go ahead in a taxi and organise some beer; the others would follow later. Edwards went along with this plan. What he did not know was that Dahmer had given his friends the wrong address.

Edwards did not like Dahmer's apartment – it smelt funny. There was a fish tank, where Dahmer kept some Siamese fighting fish. Dahmer told lurid tales about the fish fighting to the death and Edwards glanced nervously at the clock as he sipped his cold beer.

When the beer was finished, Dahmer gave Edwards a rum-and-Coke; it was drugged. Edwards became drowsy. Dahmer put his arms around him and whispered about going to bed. Instantly, Edwards was wide awake. It was all a mistake. He had to be going, he said.

Before he knew it, he was handcuffed and Dahmer was poking a butcher's knife in his chest, ordering him to get undressed. Edwards realised the seriousness of his situation. He knew he had to humour the man and make him relax. Slowly, he unbuttoned his shirt.

Dahmer suggested that they go through into the bedroom and escorted Edwards there at knifepoint. The room was decorated with Polaroid pictures of young men posing naked. There were other pictures of dismembered bodies and chunks of meat. The smell in the room was sickening. The putrid aroma seemed to be coming from a plastic dust-bin under the window. Edwards could guess the rest.

Dahmer wanted to watch a video with his captive friend.

They sat on the bed and watched *The Exorcist*. The grue-some film made Dahmer relax and Edwards desperately thought of ways to escape.

The film over, Dahmer said that if Edwards did not comply with his requests, he would cut out his heart and eat it. Then he told Edwards to strip so that he could photograph him nude. As Dahmer reached for the camera, Edwards seized his opportunity. He punched him in the side of the head. As Dahmer went down, Edwards kicked him in the stomach and ran for the door.

Dahmer caught up with him and offered to unlock the handcuffs, but Edwards ignored him. He wrenched open the door and ran for his life.

Halfway down 25th Street, Edwards spotted a police car. He ran over to it yelling for help. In the car, he explained to the officer that a maniac had tried to kill him and he directed them back to Dahmer's apartment.

The door was answered by a well-groomed white man who seemed calm and composed. The police began to have second thoughts about the story Edwards had told them – until they noticed the strange smell.

Dahmer admitted that he had threatened Edwards. He looked contrite and explained that he had just lost his job and had been drinking. But when the police asked for the key to the handcuffs, he refused to hand it over and grew violent. The policemen pushed him back into the flat and, in moments, had him face down on the floor. They read him his rights. Then they began looking around the flat. One of them opened the fridge door.

'Oh my God,' he said, 'there's a goddamn head in here.'

Dahmer began to scream like an animal. The police rushed out to get some shackles. Then they began their search of the apartment in earnest.

The refrigerator contained meat, including a human heart, in plastic bags. There were three human heads in the freezer. A filing cabinet contained grotesque photographs, three human skulls and a collection of bones. Two more skulls were found in a pot on the stove. Another pot contained male genital organs and severed hands and there were the remains of three male torsos in the dustbin in the bedroom.

In the precinct, Dahmer seemed almost relieved that his murder spree was over. He made a detailed confession and admitted that he had now reached the stage where he was cooking and eating his victims' bodies.

He also admitted to killing a teenage hitch-hiker when he was 18. When he was shown a missing-persons picture of Steven Hicks, he identified him as the person he had killed. The back garden at West Bath Road was dug up while officers sprayed Luminol mist into the crawl space. Thirteen years after the event, an eerie green handprint glowed on the cinder block wall and an outline of a pool of green – dried blood – glowed in the shadows.

A 25-man team raked the soil in the back garden, inch by inch, searching for bone fragments. The remains of Steven Hicks were unearthed and collected. The police dug down 2in–6in into the rocky soil, sifting the earth to yield more fragments. After a week, they had inventoried 593 individual items including bone fragments, pieces of two incisors, a fragment of a molar, finger bones and other shards.

They were then pieced painstakingly together by anthropologist C Owen Lovejoy, famed for his reconstruction of 'Lucy', thought to be an early ancestor of humans. It was important to establish that only one victim's bones had been scattered in the backyard.

The Summit County Coroner William A Cox was also on the case. A forensic pathologist, he had been head of pathology at the Westover Air Force Base Hospital in Massachusetts. Later, he studied at the Smithsonian Institute and the Armed Forces Institute of Pathology, where military specialists were trained to identify the battlefield dead from the smallest fragment.

'Everything we do is to make a scientific determination,' said Cox. 'But at the same time, you keep in the back of your mind that this was once a living, breathing human being. There are people out there who loved him. The family has asked for the remains to be returned back to them. And we're going to do that, so they can pay their last respects.'

Fortunately, the Hicks family had saved some of their son's hair. With this, it was possible to make a genetic match to the remains.

Dahmer's cannibalism and his necrophilia were the cornerstones of his insanity plea. But the District Attorney pointed out to the jury that if Dahmer were found insane and sent to a mental hospital, his case would be reviewed in two years and, if he was then found to be sane, he could be out on the streets again. The jury found Jeffrey Dahmer guilty of the 15 murders he was charged with and he was given 15 life sentences, or 957 years in prison. The state of Wisconsin had no death penalty, but he still faced execution. He still had to be tried for the murder that took place in his parents' home in Ohio, which did have the death penalty. He was later sentenced to life imprisonment there, too. However, after serving two years in the state penitentiary, he was murdered by another inmate.

5

BACK OF
THE BOARDING
HOUSE

In November 1988, Detective John Cabrera visited the boarding house at 1426 F Street in Sacramento, California, with a team of investigators. They were looking for 51-year-old Alvaro 'Bert' Montoya, a schizophrenic with learning difficulties. He had been a tenant there and his social worker had reported him missing.

The two-storey weatherboard Victorian house stood in a quiet, tree-lined street in what had once been an upmarket area of the state capital. The old governor's mansion was only two blocks away. But the neighbourhood had seen better times; most of the once-desirable family homes had been boarded up or were used as cheap flop houses.

The owner of 1426, Mrs Dorothea Puente, rented out rooms to the elderly and infirm. The pale-blue house was known to give off a putrid odour that the 59-year-old boarding-house mistress blamed on the sewer getting backed up or, on other occasions, dead rats rotting under the floorboards or the fish emulsion she used to fertilise the back garden. To hide the smell, she sprayed her parlour with a lemon-scented air-freshener. She also dumped gallons of bleach and bags of lime in the back garden.

As Detective Cabrera approached the house, he noticed that it was already strung with Christmas lights although it was only 11 November. Otherwise, behind its black iron fence and lace curtains, the place looked shabby, but genteel.

Cabrera knocked on the front door and asked Puente whether he could have a look around. She told him to go ahead. The place was full of porcelain dolls, doilies, vases and other knick-knacks an old lady might collect.

In the backyard, he discovered that the soil in one corner had recently been disturbed. The police team had brought spades and shovels with them and returned to their cars to get them. They began digging and quickly came across what Cabrera said looked like 'shreds of cloth and beef jerky'. Further progress was hindered by what appeared to be the root of a tree. When they could not shift it, Cabrera climbed down into the hole.

'I wrapped my hand around it, braced my feet and started pulling,' Cabrera told the *Sacramento Bee*. 'I pulled so hard that it broke loose, and when I pulled it up, I could see the joint. It was a bone ... at that time, I was airborne and out of the hole.'

Puente came out of the house to see what the commotion was about. When she was told that they had found what appeared to be human remains, she appeared shocked and slapped the sides of her face with her palms. Next, they unearthed a shoe with a foot still in it.

The following morning, a team of forensic anthropologists, officials from the coroner's office and a crew with a mechanical digger arrived. They completed the excavation of the body the police officers had partially unearthed the day before. It was little more than a skeleton and belonged to a small white-haired female.

A crowd of onlookers gathered outside the black iron fence and small boys climbed the trees to get a better view. There was a party atmosphere until a second body was found. As it was carried out to the coroner's wagon, the crowd fell silent.

Further work was hampered by a concrete slab. As workmen took a drill to it, Mrs Puente appeared. She was wearing a bright red overcoat, purple pumps and was carrying a pink umbrella. She asked Cabrera whether she was under arrest. When he said no, she asked if she could go and have a cup of coffee in the Clarion Hotel nearby. He then escorted her through the crowd of reporters who had now turned up, before returning to the excavation.

Three more bodies were found under the concrete slab and there was another one under the gazebo. Four hours had passed before anyone noticed that Mrs Puente had not returned.

In all, seven bodies were found in Puente's back garden. Alvaro Montoya, who had argued in Spanish with the voices inside his head and called Puente 'Mama', was found under a newly planted apricot tree.

BACK OF THE BOARDING HOUSE

Fifty-five-year-old alcoholic Benjamin Fink was found dressed in striped boxer shorts. Shortly before he had disappeared in April 1988, Puente told another boarder that she was going to 'take Ben upstairs and make him feel better'.

Sixty-two-year-old James Gallop had survived a heart attack and surgery to remove a brain tumour – but wasn't so resilient during his stay on F Street. He was last seen in July 1987 when he told his doctor that he was moving to 1426.

Sixty-four-year-old Native American Dorothy Miller had a drinking problem and liked to recite poems about heartbreak. She was found with her arms taped to her chest with duct tape. The last time her social worker saw her, she was sitting on the front porch, smoking a cigarette.

Vera Faye Martin was also 64; she had moved in in October 1987. Her wristwatch was still ticking when she was dug up.

Seventy-eight-year-old Betty Palmer was found in a sleeveless white nightgown below a statue of St Francis of Assisi, a few feet from the sidewalk. Her head, hands and lower legs were missing.

Leona Carpenter was also 78; she had been discharged from the hospital to Puente's care in February 1987, before disappearing a few weeks later. Buried near the back fence, it had been her leg bone that Detective Cabrera had mistaken for a tree root.

The bodies were all in an advanced state of decay. Their internal organs had fused together in a single leather mass. Police clerk Joy Underwood, who had been sent to the morgue one night to label evidence, was so distressed by the state of the bodies that she vomited every time she saw a news report about the case and began to shower compulsively.

'I still have the taste of death in my mouth,' she told Associated Press six months later. 'I can't eat vegetables grown in the ground because they have dirt around them, like the people dug up in Puente's yard – and I'm a vegetarian.'

Police searched in the boarding house and found a note. Against the first initial of each victim, Puente had written the amount she got from fraudulently cashing their Social Security and disability cheques. According to the *Sacramento Bee*, she was making $5,000 a month from the dead tenants in the back garden. She was also making a good income from her living tenants. They were paying $350 a month for a private room and two hot meals a day. Breakfast was at 6.30am sharp and consisted of eggs, bacon and pancakes. There was a second big meal at 3.30pm. Lateness was not tolerated; if residents missed either meal, they went hungry. They were not allowed near the kitchen at other hours, nor were they allowed to touch the tele-phone or the mail.

In Mrs Puente's second-storey apartment, the police found silk dresses and $110 bottles of Giorgio perfume. It was also noted that she had just had a facelift.

While drinking was strictly forbidden for residents, Mrs Puente kept a well-stocked liquor cabinet for herself upstairs. In the evenings, she would ply for trade around the seedy bars, buying drinks for lonely old men and enquiring about their financial situation. If they could afford her rents, she would ask them to become a tenant.

'She asked me where I got my money from, where I was working,' said 67-year-old John Terry, a regular at nearby Harry's Bar. 'About every time she would see me, she'd hit me up about it, wanting me to move in.'

He refused and lived to tell the tale.

With Puente on the run, the police and journalists tried to build up a picture of her. Sixty-four-year-old retired cook John Sharp, who had lived in Puente's boarding house for eleven months, said that, although she could be a martinet, she had her kinder side. She took in stray cats and bought her boarders clothes and cigarettes. She even bought one disabled tenant a tricycle so they could get round more and, at Christmas, handed out tamales (a Mexican dish). The reporter from *National Enquirer* asked whether the meat in the tamales tasted funny.

Puente had befriended 54-year-old cab driver Patty Casey. He ran errands for her several times a week – buying cement, plants or fertiliser, or dropping her off at dive bars in downtown Sacramento. She had even told him about her recent facelift. She also admitted that she was really 71, not 59 as the records said, and that she had four failed marriages behind her.

'I thought she was a nice person,' Casey told the *LA Times*. 'I really looked up to her and admired her. I felt I could learn a few things from her. I thought she was very savvy.' When he visited the boarding house, he noticed the smell, but accepted her explanation about dead rats rotting under the floorboards.

The tenants were interviewed. They had noticed that, several times when a tenant had gone missing, Puente had said they were unwell and she was 'taking them upstairs to make them feel better'. She had a variety of excuses for their absence. One tenant, she said, was becoming burdensome and 'telling her how to run her house'. So she had packed his stuff into cardboard boxes in the middle of the night and thrown them on the street. Another left suddenly to live out of state with relatives.

Posing under the guise of a harmless old lady, Puente had been a lifelong criminal. The records, at least, say that she was born Dorothea Helen Gray on 9 January 1929. She claimed to have been the youngest of 18 children. Her birth certificate shows that she was her mother's sixth child.

Her father died of tuberculosis when she was eight; her mother was killed in a motorcycle accident the following year. She had been sent to an orphanage until relatives in Fresno took her in. Later, she said she was one of three children, born and raised in Mexico.

According to relatives, the Gray children were farmed out to different homes. The census records that she lived in the city of Napa at the age of 13. School records show she was a student in Los Angeles when she turned 16. Soon after, she moved to Olympia, Washington, where she called herself 'Sheri' and worked in a milkshake parlour there in the summer of 1945. She and a friend were living in a motel room and turning tricks as prostitutes.

That autumn, she met 22-year-old Fred McFaul, a soldier who had just returned from the war in the Philippines. 'She was a good-looking female,' McFaul told the *Bee*. 'She knew how to make a buck when she wanted to.'

They married in Reno a few months later. The 16-year-old Dorothea Gray called herself 'Sherriale A Riscile' on the marriage certificate and said she was 30.

Indeed, she was an inveterate liar. She claimed to have survived through the Bataan Death March, a three-month forced march of American and Filipino prisoners of war in the Second World War which occurred when she was 13, and the dropping of the atomic bomb on Hiroshima in 1945. She was nowhere near Japan at the time. Her brother, she told people, was the US ambassador to Sweden, and she was a close friend of Rita Hayworth. To live up to the image, she loved to adorn her body with expensive clothes – silk stockings and provocative dresses.

She and McFaul set up home in Gardnerville, Nevada, where she had two daughters. Shortly after the birth of the second girl, she went to Los Angeles; she was pregnant several months later. She miscarried the baby, but McFaul left her anyway – she later claimed that he died of a heart attack in the early days of their marriage. One of their daughters was raised by his mother; the other was adopted.

Dorothea McFaul returned to prostitution, supplementing her earnings with petty crime. In 1948, she stole cheques from an acquaintance to buy a hat, purse, shoes and stockings. She was convicted of forgery, served four years in jail, then skipped town while she was still on probation. Soon, she was pregnant by a man she barely knew and gave that child up for adoption, too.

In 1952, she married her second husband, Axel Johansson, a merchant seaman. When he returned from long absences, he would sometimes find his wife living with another man and neighbours complained of taxis dropping off strange men at all hours of the night. Nevertheless, their turbulent marriage lasted for 14 years.

In 1960, she was convicted of residing in a brothel in Sacramento. She told authorities she was just visiting a friend there, and did not know that the place was a whorehouse. She served 90 days in Sacramento County Jail, then another 90 for vagrancy. After she was released, she worked as a nurse's aide, looking after elderly and disabled people in private homes. Then she started managing boarding houses.

During 1968, she opened a halfway house for alcoholics called 'The Samaritans'. Divorced from Johansson, at 39, she married 21-year-old Robert José Puente. The couple argued constantly and the marriage ended a year later. By then, the halfway house was closed after running up $10,000 in debt.

Soon after, she took over the boarding house at 2100 F Street in Sacramento and, in 1976, she married one of the tenants, 52-year-old Pedro Angel Montalvo, a violent alcoholic. 'She wanted new pantyhose every day,' complained Montalvo. 'She thought she was rich.' The marriage only lasted a few months and she retained the name from her former marriage – Puente.

In 1978, she was convicted of forging 34 cheques she had stolen from her tenants. She served five years on probation and was ordered to undergo counselling. A psychiatrist who interviewed her diagnosed her as a schizophrenic and a 'very disturbed woman'.

Then in 1981, she began renting an upstairs apartment in 1426 F Street. The following spring, 61-year-old Ruth Munroe moved in, bringing with her $6,000 in cash and all her earthly belongings. She was Puente's friend and a business partner in a small lunchroom. Her husband was terminally ill in a Veterans Administration Hospital.

Munroe was optimistic about their business, which seemed to offer a way forward. But two weeks after moving in with Puente, she began to feel ill. She told a friend she met in a beauty parlour that she felt she was going die, although she did not know why. Three days later, Munroe died of an overdose of codeine and Tylenol. Puente told the police that she had been depressed because of her husband's illness. The coroner ruled that her death was suicide.

Just a month later, Puente was arrested and charged with drugging four elderly people and stealing their valuables. One of the victims, 74-year-old pensioner Malcolm McKenzie, told the *Sacramento Bee* that Puente doped him, then looted his home as he watched in a stupor, unable to speak or move.

The judge sentenced Puente to five years in the California Institution for Women at Frontera. She was released after three years, in 1985, and ordered to not 'handle government cheques of any kind issued to others' and to stay away from the elderly.

She violated this parole condition before she had left prison when she began corresponding with a 77-year-old pen pal from Oregon named Everson Gillmouth, who told Puente he had a good pension and owned a trailer.

When Puente left jail after serving just three years of her sentence, Gillmouth was waiting at the gates in a 1980 red Ford pickup. They moved back into the apartment at 1426 F Street, paying $600 a month rent. Gillmouth had told his sister he was going to marry Puente, and that they had opened a joint account.

In November 1985, Puente gave handyman Ismael Florez a 1980 red Ford pickup, saying that it belonged to her boyfriend in Los Angeles who no longer needed it. She then asked him to build her a box 6ft x 3ft x 2ft to store books. When it was filled and nailed shut, he was to help her take it to the storage depot. On the way, she changed her mind and they dumped it on the banks of the Sacramento River. Three months later, Puente sent a card to Everson's sister saying 'Thinking of You'. She later told his sister they were in the room-and-board business, but Everson had not contacted her because he was ill.

Gillmouth's remains were found in their makeshift coffin by a fisherman in January 1986, but would lay unidentified for another three years in the city morgue. Meanwhile, Puente went on collecting Gillmouth's pension.

When the owner of 1426 F Street moved out, Puente took over. She arranged to take in homeless clients, but she did not tell the social workers about her five felony convictions for drugging and robbing the elderly. And nobody at Social Services did their homework.

Puente accepted the hardest clients to place – drug

addicts and alcoholics, and people who were violent or verbally abusive. One former social worker told the *Bee* she had put 19 senior citizens in Puente's care between 1987–88, because 'Dorothea was the best the system had to offer'.

But the Social Services were not the only ones at fault. Federal parole agents visited Puente 15 times in the two years leading up to the discovery in the backyard and never realised she was running a boarding house for the elderly – in direct violation of her parole.

An independent county agency published a reported called *Sins of Omission*. It criticised the Sacramento Police Department's handling of the case as well as that of another ten public and private agencies that had dealings with the boarding house.

One of the Sacramento Police Department's biggest failings was to allow Puente to walk out of 1426 F Street to get a cup of coffee at the Clarion Hotel two blocks away. While she drank her coffee, she called a cab, which took her to a bar on the other side of town. There she chugged down four vodkas and grapefruit, before catching another taxi to Stockton and boarding a bus for Los Angeles.

A few days later, 59-year-old retired carpenter Charles Willgues was nursing a mid-afternoon beer at the Monte Carlo tavern in downtown Los Angeles when a stranger in a bright red overcoat took the stool next to him. She seemed familiar.

She ordered a vodka and orange juice and introduced herself as Donna Johansson. She said she was from Sacramento and her husband had recently died. The grieving widow was hoping to begin a new life in LA, but things had got off to a bad start. The cabbie who had dropped her off at the $25-a-night Royal Viking Motel had driven off with her suitcases, and the heels of her only remaining pair of shoes were broken. Leaning back on her bar stool, she showed him the damaged purple shoe, along with a flash of ankle.

Feeling sorry for the woman, Willgues took her shoe to the cobbler across the street and had it repaired. His grateful companion then asked him how much money he got from Social Security a month. He told her – $576. She then said she was a good cook and suggested they move in together. After all, they were two lonely souls, so why not keep each other company?

'I've got all I can handle right now,' he said, somewhat taken aback. But he agreed to take her for a chicken dinner at a fast-food joint and arranged to go shopping with her the next day to replace the items the cabbie had stolen. Back in his apartment, Willgues switched on the television to see a picture of his companion, along with some footage of bodies being disinterred from her back garden. He called the local TV station, who in turn called the police.

'I'm just very thankful that the relationship didn't go any further,' Willgues told the *LA Times*.

At 10.40pm, Los Angeles police surrounded the motel where Puente was staying, and she was arrested. During the flight back to Sacramento, she told one reporter, 'I have not killed anyone. The cheques I cashed, yes ... I used to be a very good person at one time.'

BACK OF THE BOARDING HOUSE

She was charged with nine counts of murder and pleaded not guilty at the Sacramento Municipal Court on 31 March 1989. It took another four years to sift the evidence. Her trial began in February 1993 and, because of the extensive pretrial publicity, the hearing was moved from Sacramento to Monterey. It took another three months to empanel (enrol) the jury of four women and eight men.

Prosecutor John O'Mara said that Puente murdered her lodgers to steal their government cheques – she had selected them deliberately. 'She wanted people who had no relatives, no friends, no family ... people who, when they're gone, won't have others coming around and asking questions,' he said.

He told the jury that Puente had used sleeping pills to knock out her victims, then suffocated them, and hired convicts to dig the holes in her garden in which to bury them.

Her defence team maintained that the tenants died of natural causes. Puente did not call paramedics to retrieve the bodies because she was running the boarding house in violation of her parole and didn't want to be sent back to prison. So she buried the bodies in her back garden.

The defence painted Puente as a benevolent soul who selflessly cared for 'the dregs of society, people who had no place else to go'. The rent she received from her tenants barely covered the operating costs. She stole money to cover her expenses, but she was not a killer.

Throughout the five months, Puente maintained the demeanour of a sweet little granny, dressing in flowery frocks. But some found this unsettling. When the prosecution showed photos of Puente's victims – first alive and smiling, then freshly disinterred from the garden – *USA Today* reported that she viewed them without flinching.

'Dorothea Puente murdered nine people,' O'Mara told jurors. 'Don't turn your back on reason.'

However, there were no eyewitnesses to the alleged murders. Apart from the case of Ruth Munroe, they could not ascertain the cause of death; the bodies were too decayed. Toxicological tests did reveal, though, that there were traces of Dalmane (flurazepam) – a prescription-strength sleeping pill – in all the remains.

Expert witnesses testified that Dalmane could be lethal, especially when taken with alcohol or other sedatives, and it was particularly potent in elderly people. At Puente's preliminary hearing, a doctor testified that Puente had used Dorothy Miller's ID card to try to get a prescription for Dalmane, but the doctor had refused her. But she had an abundant supply; Dalmane was given to her by her court-appointed psychiatrist and she got it from two other doctors as well.

Former tenant Carol Durning testified that James Gallop complained that Puente was giving him drugs that made him sleep all the time. She had also overheard Puente telling him he would have to leave unless he let her take charge of his money.

And Alvaro 'Bert' Montoya complained to William Johnson, an employee of a local detox centre where he lived before moving to 1426 F Street, that Puente was 'giving him a medicine he didn't like to take'. When Johnson confronted Puente, she flew into a rage and told him to take Montoya back to the detox centre if he was going to meddle in her business. But Johnson advised Montoya to stay at the boarding house where he would be better off.

'I told him, "You'll be safe there,"' Johnson told the court. 'I was wrong … I've got to live with this for the rest of my life.'

After Montoya was dead, Puente paid Donald Anthony, a local halfway house resident, to call Montoya's social worker, posing as his brother-in-law, and say that Montoya had gone to live with his family out of state. But Anthony had mistakenly used his own name when he left the message on the social worker's answering machine. It was this blunder that led Detective Cabrera to take an interest in Puente's boarding house.

A handwriting expert confirmed that Puente had signed the names of seven dead tenants on sixty federal and state cheques that were sent to 1426 F Street. But Puente was not charged with forgery; the prosecution thought the additional charge would make the case too complex for jurors.

They also produced handyman Ismael Florez who testified about dumping Everson Gillmouth's body by the Sacramento River. Again, Puente was not charged with Gillmouth's murder as the statute of limitations had been exceeded.

Homer Myers, who had been a tenant for two years after she picked him up in a bar, said he unwittingly dug one of the victims' graves. He said Puente had told him to dig a 4-ft hole to plant a small apricot tree. He had wondered why she had wanted it so deep. He then refused to sign docu-ments empowering her to cash his social security cheques. That saved his life.

The jurors were taken on a tour of Sacramento. They visited the seedy bars where she trawled for victims. They were taken to the house, then they walked about the back garden where Puente had planted flowers over the corpses. By that time, it was dark.

'You can't see much back there,' said juror Joe Martin. 'But you feel a lot. It's weird.'

The trial had taken a year and the jury, after being out for a month, found Puente guilty on three counts of murder – Dorothy Miller, Benjamin Fink and Leona Carpenter. They were then asked to consider the sentence. O'Mara said that the jury must think of the victims – 'These people were human beings, they had a right to live. They did not have a lot of possessions – no houses, no cars, only their social security cheques and their lives. She took it all … Death is the only appropriate penalty.'

Her defence attorney Kevin Clymo said, 'I think you can only truly understand why so many people testified and asked you to spare Dorothea's life only if you have ever fallen down and stumbled on the road of life and had someone pick you up, give you comfort, give you love, show you the way. Then you will understand why these people believe Dorothea's life is worth saving. That is mitigating. That is a human quality that deserves to be preserved. It is a flame of humanity that has burned inside Dorothea since she was young ... That is the reason to give Dorothea Puente life without the possibility of parole.'

After the jury was deadlocked, she was spared. One juror said, 'Executing Puente would be like executing your grandma.'

Puente was given two life sentences without the possibility of parole along with a concurrent 15-year-to-life sentence. She died in prison in Chowchilla, California – on 27 March 2011, at the age of 82 – from natural causes, still protesting her innocence.

Her former boarding house – and its garden – were open to the public as a grim spectacle in 2013. It featured a mannequin dressed in Puente's red coat, holding a shovel. Among those who have taken the tour when it opened was Detective Cabrera, who had since retired.

'I wanted to come back when the house is redone, when it's happy,' Cabrera said. 'I'm grateful that now the community can come and see it.'

He pointed out where the bodies and evidence were found. Giving local TV station KCRA a guided tour, he said, 'And this is what we would call "The Death Room". This is where she brought her victims, after she had induced drugs or alcohol. And she would place them here on the floor, and they would lay here for up to days or weeks, we don't know.'

It was there that she let their bodily fluids drain. Cabrera found the blankets, sheets and plastic sheeting pile up. She used them to wrap the bodies.

'There was a bookshelf and a day bed,' he recalled. 'The room had two carpets and I pulled the carpet and saw there were stains. I knew right away it was body fluid.'

The back stairs led from the rear of her bathroom. Puente used these to carry the bodies down to the back garden. Cabrera thought that someone helped her do this. At the time, another resident was arrested, but later released. He also said that Puente had hired parolees to dig holes in the yard for her, telling them that she needed to have new plants in the garden.

'She was an ex-con hiring ex-cons,' he said.

In the back garden, he pointed out where Montoya's fully clothed body was found near the back fence. Another was unearthed close to what is now the step of a new shed; a third body was found underneath a timber outhouse. Tickets for the tour sold for $20–$30.

Cabrera told the *Sacramento Bee* that he was impressed with the renovations that had been done to the house. 'I'm very happy to be back and happy to see the changes,' he said. 'I love this house. It's happy. This veil of darkness has been lifted.'

One visitor, 65-year-old Susan Fishel of Sacramento said, 'I think you have to have a sense of humour if you're going to live in a place like this.'

6

AUSSIE RULES

On 20 May 1999, the sleepy bush town of Snowtown, South Australia, came to world attention when the police entered a disused redbrick building on Main Street. It had once been the Snowtown branch of the State Bank of South Australia which, like many rural branches, had long been closed. What led them there was a year-long investigation of the state's growing number of missing person cases. Behind the 4-in steel door of the bank's vault, they found six black plastic barrels that gave off a stomach-churning smell. The acid-filled drums contained partly dissolved human body parts. Among them were 15 feet, leading the police to conclude that the drums contained the remains of at least eight murder victims.

The following day, three homes in a blue-collar area nearby were raided. Three men were arrested and charged with the murder of an unknown number of people between

1 August 1993 and 20 May 1999. They were 40-year-old Mark Haydon of Smithfield Plains; 32-year-old former abattoir worker John Bunting of Craigmore; and 27-year-old Robert Wagner of Elizabeth Grove. They were denied bail. Meanwhile, the police, convinced there were more bodies, continued their search.

They were contacted by Wally Fitzgerald who called the Crime Stoppers line, alerting them to secret suburban graves. Fitzgerald was a friend of 19-year-old James (Jamie) Vlassakis; Bunting had offered a helping hand to Jamie.

But Jamie soon became aware of Bunting's darker side. While ranting about paedophiles, Bunting would skin animals alive for fun. Gradually, Vlassakis had been drawn into Bunting's circle and began taking heroin in an effort to block out what he had witnessed. When Bunting had been arrested, a distraught Vlassakis had turned to Fitzgerald for emotional support and told him that bodies were buried in the backyard of the house where Bunting used to live.

On 23 May, a task force of officers under Detective Sergeant Brian Swan arrived at 203 Waterloo Corner Road in North Salisbury, Adelaide, the site of Bunting's old semi-detached house which had since been demolished. The police were convinced that the house, though flattened, might still yield vital evidence, and they brought with them sophisticated ground-penetrating radar equipment, first developed to detect plastic landmines laid during the Falklands War. Similar equipment had been used to scan the garden at Fred and Rosemary West's 'House of Horrors' in Cromwell Street, Gloucester.

First, a large tent was erected in the back garden, covering the detectives' area of interested. Three inches below the surface in the corner of the yard, there was a concrete slab that had once supported a rainwater tank. The technicians rolled the radar detector over the area and found that there was something down there.

Officers began digging. They used sledgehammers and crowbars to break up the concrete slab, and kept digging through the compacted earth below. It took them five hours to get down another 4ft. There they caught sight of a green garbage bag. As they proceeded cautiously, they discovered another ten garbage bags. One of them was opened, releasing the stench of rotting flesh. Inside were what appeared to be human remains.

The bags were tagged, photographed and taken to the Forensic Science Centre in Adelaide, where they were X-rayed by Dr Roger Byard. Inside one bag he found a human torso with some of the internal organs attached; the skin had been stripped off. The chest had been crushed and the genitals were missing. The feet were found in another bag, along with the head. A length of blue nylon rope was tangled in the hair. The arms, hands and legs were in other bags. The skin had again been stripped from the limbs with a knife. A knife had also been used to disarticulate the joints. When the body was reconstructed, it was clear that all the body parts found belonged to one individual, an adult white female.

Three days later, the task force returned to the backyard of 203 Waterloo Road. Digging down a further 6ft, they found a skeleton. The bones were removed one by one, along with the hood of a khaki parka that covered the skull. None of the bones were broken. No ligature was present and no cause of death could be discerned. The death toll was now in double figures.

The police missing-persons' task force, codenamed Chart, had initially been set up to investigate the disappearance of just three people – 22-year-old Clinton Trezise, who disappeared in 1993; his friend, the 40-year-old flamboyant transvestite and convicted paedophile Barry Lane – aka Vanessa – who went missing in October 1997; and 37-year-old mother of eight Elizabeth Haydon, who had vanished earlier that year. She was the wife of the accused, Mark Haydon, whose car had led the now 33-man police task force to the bank building in Snowtown. Cars from out of town tend to attract attention in a small community like Snowtown and sightings of the other unfamiliar vehicles had led detectives to the other suspects.

The barrels found in Snowtown had done the rounds before ending up in the bank vault there. They had first been kept in a shed behind Bunting's house in Murray Bridge in April 1998. Three were then moved to Haydon's house at Smithfield Plains. Later, one was stored in the back of a Mitsubishi Sigma at Murray Bridge, while five were kept in the back of a Toyota Land Cruiser at Hoyleton on the Adelaide Plains. They were moved to the bank after complaints about the smell. The accused had claimed that they contained kangaroo meat.

Forensic scientists had the distasteful task of trying to

identify the victims from their dental records and fingerprints. This was difficult as the body parts were partially dissolved. So the, then new, and expensive technique of DNA profiling was used. Even body parts that had been left dissolving in acid for some time rendered useful DNA that could be extracted and compared with hair from combs of suspected victims or samples taken from their soiled clothing. It transpired that some of the victims were collecting Disability Support Benefit and the authorities had not been informed of their deaths. And others, who had formally been declared dead, were still, apparently, collecting their benefits.

There may have been other motives for the killings. The accused, Robert Wagner, was a white supremacist and a vociferous hater of homosexuals. But the primary reason for the murders was financial – the killers were drawing AUS$100,000 a year intended for their dead victims.

Meanwhile, the police were interviewing James Vlassakis; he was feeling the pressure. In a taped phone call played at the trial, he told his teenage girlfriend Amanda Warwick about the bodies in the barrels and said that he would soon be arrested. She asked if he had anything to do with the murders. He replied, 'It's too big, I can't tell you.'

Vlassakis was not cautioned. He was told that, as a result, any statement he made could not be used against him in court. It would be forwarded to the Director of Public Prosecutions, where it would be checked for accuracy. Only then would the decision be made to offer him full immunity.

The interrogation continued for the next ten days. During that time, Vlassakis frequently broke down. He overdosed on heroin and nearly died. Then he cracked and told the detective a harrowing tale of ritualistic torture and murder, sometimes with music playing in the background. Vlassakis related how much Bunting and Wagner enjoyed the pain and suffering they were inflicting. Bunting liked to stare into the eyes of a victim who knew they were about to die. He also described the kick Bunting got when the true-crime show *Australia's Most Wanted* reported the discovery of a skeleton at a place called Lower Light, 20 miles north of Adelaide. The case remained unsolved, but Bunting announced, with excitement, 'That's my handiwork.'

The interview finished on 2 June 1999. Afterwards, James Vlassakis was arrested. Initially, he was only charged with just one murder that had taken place on 4 May 1999, although the name of the victim was suppressed. After his arrest, Vlassakis repeatedly attempted suicide and was moved from prison to the secure wing of a psychiatric hospital.

Another house in Murray Bridge was raided and an 11th body was unearthed. The police then went through their 'unsolved crimes' file and tied the current murder investigation to the bones found in the field at Lower Light in 1994 and the body of a man found hanging from a tree in 1997. Initially, his death was thought to have been a suicide, but he was later implicated in the murder of Barry Lane. Gavin Porter, a missing man from the neighbouring state of Victoria, also appeared to be a victim and the police began to suspect that the gang's murder spree had begun in 1992.

More properties were raided in the wheat belt around Snowtown and along the Murray River and there was press speculation that the gang extended much further that the four already in custody. Indeed, the gang had once been bigger. It became clear that some of the victims had once been perpetrators. The gang had turned in on itself and began killing its own. The transvestite Barry Lane had lived with the accused Robert Wagner – a neo-Nazi who, purportedly, hated Asians and gays – just a block away from Bunting's demolished house where the two corpses had been unearthed. They were on Disability Support, like many of the victims.

It was suspected that Lane had had a hand in the murder of his boyfriend Clinton Trezise. His were the bones found in Lower Light in 1994 and eventually identified by comparison with an X-ray held by a former employer. Trezise had been butchered in Bunting's living room in Salisbury North. Bunting had also been engaged to Gail Sinclair, sister of the murder victim Elizabeth Haydon, Mark Haydon's wife.

The four accused went on trial in November 2000. Bunting, Wagner and Haydon were charged with ten counts of murder, but remained silent and refused to plead. Vlassakis, then charged with five counts of murder, reserved his plea. The evidence given in court was so gruesome that suppression orders were used to keep much of it from the public. The Snowtown murder case was subjected to over

150 suppression orders in all, some of which have not been lifted. However, some of the horrendous details were reported by newspapers in the UK.

While the prosecution asserted that the murders had been carried out as part of a benefit fraud, the *Daily Telegraph* revealed that the victims had been sadistically tortured. Some victims had burn marks on their bodies; others had ropes around their necks. Several were gagged and one died with his legs tied together and his arms handcuffed behind his back. A machine that delivered electric shocks was found in the bank vault in Snowtown, along with rubber gloves, ropes, tape, handcuffs, knives and a bloodstained saw. One victim had received electric shocks to the penis and testicles. A burning sparkler had been push into his urethra. His nose and ears were burnt with cigarettes and his toes were crushed before he was left to choke to death on his gag. Another had been put in a bath and assaulted with clubs. He had been beaten around the genitals and had had his toes crushed with pincers, before being garrotted with a length of rope and a tyre lever.

Victims' bodies had been mutilated and dismembered. Mrs Haydon had had her head and arms cut off; her torso had been stripped of its flesh and her breasts and genitals removed. The final victim, David Johnson, had been cooked and partially eaten.

Before they died, victims had been forced to call their tormentors 'Lord Sir', 'Chief Inspector', 'Master' and 'God'. They had also been forced to record carefully scripted phrases, which were then left on the telephone answering machines of friends and relatives to allay suspicion. Gang members then impersonated their victims at benefit offices to collect their money.

In July 2002, Vlassakis pleaded guilty to four counts of murder and was given a life sentence with the stipulation that he would serve 26 years before he was eligible for parole; he had struck a deal with the prosecution. Otherwise, he would have had to serve 42 years before he was eligible. By then, the charges against Bunting, Wagner and Haydon had increased to 12 counts of murder.

On 8 September 2003, after an 11-month trial in front of the South Australian Supreme Court, Wagner was found guilty of the murder of seven people, on top of the three murders he had admitted to earlier; Bunting was convicted of eleven murders. The jury was hung on a 12th charge – the murder of 47-year-old Suzanne Allen, whose body had been found wreathed in plastic under Bunting's demolished house. The defence claimed that she had died of natural causes.

Many of the charges against Haydon had been dropped due to lack of evidence. He was not convicted of any of the murders, but pleaded guilty to having helped dispose of the bodies. Both Wagner and Bunting refused to stand when the judgment was read, while Bunting protested loudly that details of the deal that Vlassakis had made in return for giving evidence against them had not been revealed to the jury, some of who had undergone counselling after hearing his testimony. Both were sentenced to life imprisonment without the possibility of parole.

Vlassakis's testimony had lasted 32 days. He had claimed that he had been dragged into the murders during the killing of his half-brother Troy Youde, stepbrother of the last Snowtown victim David Johnson. He vomited when he recalled how he had found Wagner cooking Johnson's flesh in a frying pan and offered him some.

The victims, Vlassakis said, were relentlessly tortured. The eighth victim, Fred Brooks, had been beaten in a bath and had had lit cigarettes stuck in his ear and nose. Wagner and Bunting, the prosecution said, boasted that 'the good ones' never screamed. Their targets, they said, were primarily homosexuals, whom they claimed to loathe.

The murders had given Snowtown a terrible notoriety. With street hawkers selling Snowtown Snow Shakers featuring body parts and barrel-shaped fridge magnets bearing the logo 'Snowtown – you'll have a barrel of fun', the inhabitants are worried that the town may never shake off its sick image. There has even been a proposal to change the name to Rosetown. Few think it will help. It would, perhaps, have been better if they had buried all the bodies in the back garden.

7

MACABRE MARGATE

In May 2007, 60-year-old Peter Tobin was found guilty of the rape and murder of 23-year-old Polish student Angelika Kluk and sentenced to life imprisonment with a minimum tariff of 21 years. Tobin was a known sex offender and it was suspected that he had been responsible for other offences, including rape and murder. Police forces across Great Britain began opening their Cold Cases files and started searching the houses Tobin had lived in.

The following month, the police searched Tobin's old home at 11 Robertson Avenue in Bathgate, West Lothian, in connection with the disappearance of 15-year-old schoolgirl Vicky Hamilton, who was last seen less than a mile away on 10 February 1991, waiting for a bus home to Redding near Falkirk.

Vicky's father, Michael, has always maintained that his daughter had not just run away. He said, 'She was a bright and bubbly teenager, tall for her age, who was starting to strike out on her own. I believe she was abducted and murdered. I hope the police will knock on my door some day soon and finally let me know what happened.'

Tobin left Bathgate soon after Vicky went missing.

After Vicky's DNA had been found at the house, the cul-de-sac was closed off and forensic specialists went to work. All the furniture of the family of three then living there was removed and the house stripped to a bare shell. Meanwhile, the police dug up the back garden and removed the wallpaper and floorboards as they conducted a meticulous search of the premises. A specialist underwater team also searched a pond at the Boghead Nature Reserve, about 500 metres from the house.

The body was not found but, on 21 July 2007, Tobin was charged in connection with Vicky Hamilton's disappearance. The search then moved south to Victoria Road North in Southsea, where Tobin lived later. Police set up a large white tent in the garden and were thought to be digging.

Nothing was found, but the police went on to search 50 Irvine Drive in Margate, another property Tobin had occupied after he left Bathgate. They dug up the garden looking as well for the body of Dinah McNicol, an 18-year-old sixth former who lived in Tillingham, Essex. She had been hitch-hiking home from a music festival in Hampshire with a boyfriend who got out at Junction 8 of the M25 near Reigate. She stayed in the car and was never seen again.

A body was found in the back garden at 50 Irvine Drive ... but it was not Dinah's. DNA tests proved that it was

Vicky Hamilton's body the police had unearthed. Her dismembered corpse was in plastic bin-bags that yielded Tobin's fingerprints. 'Intimate' swabs found traces of what appeared to be semen. The DNA matched Tobin's. A knife was then found in the loft at Robertson Avenue, that carried a tiny fragment of skin on its underside. This yielded a partial DNA match to Vicky. The chances that it had come from anyone else were one in a million.

The police continued digging up the garden at 50 Irvine Drive and, a week later, found the body of Dinah in a shallow grave just yards away from Vicky's. Both bodies contain traces of amitriptyline. This would have made the girls drowsy and dizzy, and unable to defend themselves against rape. While Dinah's green jacket and sleeveless vest were in place, her green trousers and knickers had been pulled down over her buttocks, indicating an attempted sexual assault.

There was a gag in her mouth and a ligature around her neck and the Home Office pathologist concluded that she had been strangled. While Vicky's body had been cut in two, Dinah's was bent double. A clothes line had been used to tie her neck to her ankles. Another cord coiled around her body. Her wrists were tied together with her leggings and her ankles were bound with her headscarf.

Again, Tobin's fingerprints were found on the bin-bags and on the tape with which he'd sealed them. Tobin was charged with the murder of both young women.

Born in Johnstone, Renfrewshire, on 27 August 1946, Tobin had a history of violent crime that stretched back over 40 years. He was sent to an approved school at the age of seven. He spent time in a young offenders' institution before serving jail terms for burglary, forgery and conspiracy. He also spent his adult life preying on vulnerable women, inflicting pain and humiliation – not just to innocent strangers, but also to each of those who were unfortunate enough to become his three wives.

Outwardly, he was charming, affable and good-looking. His smart suits and flattery swept women off their feet. But after the relationship developed, it was a different story. Former wives and girlfriends described him as a monster who sought to take total control of their lives, isolating them from their friends and family while mocking them in front of his.

His first wife, clerk-typist Margaret Mackintosh, was 17 when she married him in Brighton in 1969. Some 40 years later, she still bore the scars of a knife attack that he made on her. Tobin had stabbed her around her vagina, leaving her bleeding heavily. The knife, he said, was 'metal Tampax'. If it had not been for the prompt action of a neighbour, she would have died.

'He raped me three or four times, enjoying my fear,' she said. 'When I put up a fight, I got a knife in my side. He left me to die on the bed. Luckily, the man living underneath saw the blood coming through the ceiling and got me to hospital.'

When she tried to leave him, he decapitated the puppy that he had bought for her. After a year, she ran off and they divorced in 1971.

Tobin met his second wife, Sylvia Jefferies, in 1973. She was then 30 and they married in a matter of weeks. They had a son and a daughter who died soon after birth. Sylvia said that she lived in a constant state of fear. 'He'd whack me so hard it would send me flying across the room,' she said. In 1976, she left with their son.

Tobin married again in 1989 at a Methodist church in Brighton. His third wife was Cathy Wilson, who, at 16, was more than 20 years his junior. They then moved to Bathgate in 1990, where he did odd jobs around the neighbourhood, usually fixing cars. They had a son, Daniel. But after two years of marriage, she found she had become a prisoner in her home. Tobin would not allow her to go outside.

'He was violent on almost a daily basis,' she said. 'He would push me against walls or put his hands round my neck for the simplest of things. If he said something and I dared to speak back or answer him in a way he thought disrespectful, he would blow up. If I made dinner and he didn't like it, he would throw the plate at me, telling me I was stupid.'

Realising that she had to escape, she waited until Tobin went out with a friend one night. 'He'd taken my car keys, house keys, money, bank books and my driving licence with him but I had a stash of grocery money he didn't know about,' she said. 'It was only £25 but it paid for a bus ticket to Brighton. Daniel and I had two hours sitting in a coach station and I was terrified he would find us and drag us back. I was literally sitting in the station crying with fear until the bus left.'

Soon after, Tobin was admitted to hospital after taking an overdose of the antidepressant amitriptyline and triazolam, which was prescribed to relieve his anxiety. He told doctors that he had tried to commit suicide because his wife and child had left him 'without warning'.

On Friday, 8 February 1991, Vicky Hamilton had left home to spend the weekend with her older sister in Livingston. There was a lot to talk about; 15-year-old Vicky had just had a pregnancy test. It had been snowing and she could have asked her father to come and collect her. But she was at an age when she was determined to be independent. She would travel back to Redding on the Sunday evening and had to change buses at Bathgate.

When she alighted there, she was not sure where to catch her connection. She asked a young man who was eating chips for directions. He thought she was in the right place, but was not sure. So Vicky went to the chip shop and asked there.

The bus stop was down the street opposite the police station, she was told. The buses to Falkirk went every hour, on the hour. She bought a bag of chips and ate them sitting on a bench on the way. Then she confirmed that she was going the right way by asking a man on his way to the video store. Several people saw her at the bus stop, but she did not get on the bus when it arrived ten minutes later. She had simply vanished. The bus stop was right around the corner from Tobin's house. Two years later, her mother died of a broken heart.

When Vicky Hamilton was reported missing, police

scoured the neighbourhood. But they did not interview Tobin; he had only recently moved into the area and kept himself to himself.

It has not been established what he did with Vicky Hamilton after he raped and killed her. It is thought that he kept her body in the cupboard under the stairs, which caused a problem when an electrician came round to rewire the house. Tobin denied him access, and a violent argument ensued.

The knife he had used to cut up his young victim to make her concealment easier was already hidden in the loft. It had been tucked out of sight between the end wall and the last ceiling joist, behind some old bell jars and at least 15ft from the entrance hatch.

Tobin was calmer a few days after the electrician called when Cathy came to collect Daniel, who had been staying over the weekend. They subsequently moved to Hampshire.

Meanwhile, Tobin was trying to lay a false trail for the police. On 21 February, 11 days after Vicky had gone missing, Tobin went to Edinburgh, taking Vicky's purse with him. It contained an identity card and numerous other things that would identify her, as well as her bus ticket from the 10 February, an address in London, a leaflet about oral contraception and a piece of paper with the word 'Samaritans' on it, along with a phone number. Tobin dropped it in the street near both the bus and railway stations. A passer-by soon spotted it and handed it in to the police. However, it was raining that day and the purse was barely wet, so they concluded it had not been on the pavement very long.

The purse was returned to Vicky's family and the police began to widen their search. They took more than 3,000 statements and interviewed over 6,500 people as far away as London and Aberdeen. With the purse, Tobin had succeeded in shifting their attention from Bathgate, although later it would count against him. DNA belonging to his son was found on it.

As it was, the very next day, he was admitted to St John's Hospital with abdominal pains. Clearly, the anxiety had been too much for him.

Once discharged, he decided to put some distance between himself and the scene of the crime and put in a request for a council swap on the grounds that his wife and son now lived on the south coast. An exchange was arranged with Peter and Hannah Hewitson, who lived in Margate. The move would take place on 22 March.

Tobin left some of his belongings with a neighbour, saying that there was not enough room in the back of his van to carry everything. When the Hewitsons arrived, they found 11 Robertson Avenue in a terrible state. They spent days cleaning the place with bleach to try and get rid of the sickly smell. Hannah's sister Doris said, 'When I helped her move to his house in Bathgate, the stench was over-powering. It smelled like someone had died there.'

Her husband Edward added, 'He couldn't get out of Bathgate fast enough. He crammed everything he owned into a van but the stuff never arrived in Margate.'

Meanwhile, Tobin arrived at 50 Irvine Drive with his secret cargo – the dismembered body of Vicky Hamilton, destined for a shallow grave in the back garden. Soon, she would be joined by another corpse.

On Saturday, 3 August 1991, Dinah McNicol met David Tremett at the Torpedo Town Festival in Liphook, Hampshire. It was a free festival whose location was only announced at the last minute to prevent the police from banning it. They spent most of the weekend together with her friends. Dinah was in party mood; she had just finished her A-levels at Chelmsford County High School for Girls. Things had not been easy after her mother had been killed in a car accident a few years earlier.

While Dinah's friends headed off, she and David decided to stay on one more night. On Monday, they set off to hitch-hike back to their homes. At a service station near the M25, they were picked up by a scruffy man in a green hatchback. Though David, who sat in the back, thought the man was a little odd, he chatted away to Dinah in the front.

The driver stopped to let David out at the turn-off for Redhill where he lived. Worried about leaving Dinah alone with a strange man, he suggested she came with him. But she was eager to get home to Tillingham and said she would be OK.

Dinah's father had been expecting her home on 5 August – she did not show up. Normally, when her plans changed, she would phone. There was no call. Then money began to disappear from her bank account. It was withdrawn in sums of up to £250 from cash machines along the south coast between Havant in Hampshire and Margate. After three weeks, her bank account was empty.

Tobin's neighbour David Martin saw Tobin digging the hole when he looked over the garden fence. Tobin told Martin that he was digging his way to Australia, joking that it was cheaper than paying the £10 fare. Then he said he was actually digging a sandpit for his son who came to visit at weekends. When he filled it in, he told Martin that a social worker had visited and told him that the sandpit was too dangerous. There had been no such visit.

Nine months later, the disappearance of Dinah McNicol featured on the TV programme *Crimewatch*. She had been missing since she had parted from David Tremett. He went to the police in Redhill, only to discover that he was the last person to see her alive – apart from the driver of the hatchback. However, the search for Dinah progressed no further.

In 1993, the American rock band Soul Asylum released 'Runaway Train'. The accompanying video included pictures of missing kids. The UK version featured Dinah McNicol and Vicky Hamilton.

Despite their acrimonious divorce, Cathy Wilson still allowed Tobin to have access to their son. Then, on 4 August 1993, when the five-year-old went to stay with his father, he walked into Tobin's room and found two 14-year-old girls, one of them unconscious.

At that time, Tobin was living in a second-floor council flat in Leigh Park, Havant, so he could be closer to the child.

The two girls had called to visit the woman next door, who was not in. They knocked on Tobin's door and asked if they could wait there. Tobin knew one of the girls and assured her that the neighbour would not be long. Daniel was playing in another room and Tobin invited them in.

He plied them with cider and vodka. One of them passed out; the other was sick. When she tried to wake her friend, Tobin threatened her with a knife and said he would kill her if she kept on crying. He forced her at knifepoint to take a cocktail of pills and wine. When she tried to make a run for it, he grabbed her by the throat. In the ensuing struggle, she managed to stab him in the leg. Hearing the rumpus, Daniel came in. The girl begged him to get help, but Tobin ushered him out. Once the girl was unconscious, Tobin raped and sodomised her.

By then it was 2.00am and he realised that a search of the flats might already be under way. He called Cathy, telling her to come and collect Daniel as he was having a heart attack. When she arrived, Tobin and Daniel were waiting at the bottom of the stairs with a bag full of things he wanted Daniel to have in case he never saw him again.

Once they were gone, Tobin went back upstairs and turned on the gas, then opened the window and escaped down the drainpipe. But his attempt to gas the victims failed. One of the girls awoke to find her jeans on the other side of the room and her knickers round her ankles. There was also a tie around her ankle and a bloody bandage around her wrist. Her friend was lying naked next to her. She fled and raised the alarm. Their ordeal had lasted 16 hours. The other girl was still unconscious when the police arrived.

A witness said that they had seen Tobin heading towards Brighton where he happened upon a group of day-trippers from the Jesus Fellowship in Warwickshire. Adopting his third wife's maiden name, he told them that he was Peter Wilson and he was homeless. They invited him back to the secluded King's House Centre, near Southam, where he found refuge. To pay for his keep, he did odd jobs around the place.

Members of the Jesus Fellowship became suspicious and, after a month, he was asked to leave. By then, he had disguised himself by growing a moustache. A few days after he left, one of the Fellowship was watching *Crimewatch* and saw a picture of the man they knew as Peter Wilson. He was arrested soon afterwards, back in Brighton.

At Winchester Crown Court, he pleaded guilty to the rape of one of the girls and the indecent assault of the other. The prosecutor, Anthony Davies, told the court, 'Tobin treated the girls as cruelly as a cat would treat a mouse.'

The judge described the attack as 'an appalling incident, I think the worst I have ever come across'.

On 18 May 1994, Tobin was sentenced to 14 years; he was released on licence after seven of them. Almost immediately, he breached the terms of the licence when he moved home without informing the police of his new address. When he was found, he was returned to prison for another three years and was put on the Sex Offenders Register when it was introduced in 2003.

After his release, Tobin returned to his native Scotland, to live in a home in Paisley. There he met 24-year-old Cheryl McLachlan. She was the girlfriend of a drinking buddy and he invited her back to his flat to watch a football match. She had visited him there before. This time, though, he was agitated. When she announced that she was leaving, he came dashing out of the kitchen with a knife in his hand. He forced her to lie on the sofa and got on top of her.

Thinking that she was going to die, she fought him off. She caught him off balance and he fell to the floor. As she fled for the door, she yelled, 'What the hell are you playing at? Put that knife down.'

He lunged at her again. This time she grabbed his wrist. In the struggle, the cushions were knocked off the sofa. Underneath, there was a tie and a belt. Plainly, Tobin had planned to tie her up, or strangle her.

Now full of adrenalin, she felt no pain when she grabbed the blade of the knife. Eluding his grasp again, she reached the door – to find it locked. So she turned to face her attacker.

'Put that thing down and let me out of here,' she said. 'Or else.'

Curiously, this took the wind out of his sails. He apologised and said he was only joking.

'I got carried away. I didn't mean any harm. I'm just a daft old boy. I've near enough given myself a heart attack,' said the 57-year-old, holding his heart.

Cheryl was not unsympathetic. He had complained of chest pain before and she found his medicine for him before leaving. She then went to the police. But when they arrived at Tobin's flat, he had made a miraculous recovery and had left. A warrant was issued for his arrest, but the police failed to trace him.

Tobin then adopted the name Pat McLaughlin and again found refuge with a religious community – this time at St Patrick's Church in Anderston. Under the 'open doors policy', they took him on as an odd-job man. There he befriended Angelika Kluk.

A devout Catholic, she was from the small town of Skoczów which is less than ten miles from the border with the Czech Republic. Money had been hard to come by in her family, so she intended to travel to Western Europe in search of a well-paid job to pay for her continued studies. While studying at Gdansk University, she had set her eyes on Scotland, reading books and articles about the country and studying pictures of the Highlands. It looked much like her homeland. And knowing the country's history and traditions, she believed she would feel at home there. A language student, she was already fluent in English.

When Poland acceded to the European Union in May 2004, she headed west with thousands of other students. While most were drawn to the bright lights of London or Manchester, she headed straight for Scotland. She found a bed in a hostel in Edinburgh and got a job as a cloakroom attendant and cleaner.

At the end of the summer, she returned home to Poland and came back to Scotland the following year. This time she went to Glasgow where she found an early-morning job as an office cleaner and an afternoon job as a chambermaid, and a flat in the Anderston district, just five minutes' walk from St Patrick's. After mass one day, she introduced herself to Father Gerry Nugent who ran the 'open doors policy' for the needy.

A few weeks later, her landlord asked her to leave. She asked Father Nugent if he knew anyone who might rent her a room. He invited her to stay in one of the rooms in the chapel house. This invited gossip. There had been rumours about him before. A good-looking man, it had been said that he had had an affair with a married woman. And in 1993, the Archdiocese of Glasgow received a call from a woman who said he had sexually assaulted her.

Now 62, Father Nugent gave Angelika the money to make a tour of Scotland and he used his credit card to buy her a £1,500 laptop so she could stay in touch with her family via email. They became close. They would exchange a hug before they retired to their separate beds. Then came a kiss on the cheek … and soon their beds were separate no longer.

The affair was also carried on in public. They would go swimming together and she would be seen walking around in just a sheer robe that left little to the imagination in front of him.

At the end of the summer, she returned to her studies in Poland. The following year, she again visited Scotland, and Father Nugent. It was as if she had never been away.

She got a job as a nanny to a wealthy Russian family. There she met Martin MacAskill, the 40-year-old owner of a chauffeuring business. They soon became lovers. As MacAskill was married, they made love in the chapel house. Soon, she was madly in love with him.

When Father Nugent found contraceptives in her bedroom, he became jealous. In her diary, Angelika condemned his drunken petulance. Then, through a text she had sent to Martin's phone, his wife Anne found out about the affair. Anne flew to Majorca to contemplate the future of their 12-year marriage and Martin went after her.

At St Patrick's, Angelika had become Tobin's 'little apprentice'. She liked to help him out and they had become firm friends. On Sunday, 24 September 2006, just a few days before she was due to return to Poland again, she was helping him paint a shed that they had built in the garage. She needed the company. Father Nugent barely spoke to her and she had not seen Martin for ten days. By then, Tobin had been working at St Patrick's for about two months and had been dreaming of having sex with Angelika ever since he had arrived.

After a tea break, they returned to the garage. Almost immediately, Tobin clubbed her on the back on the head. As she lay on the floor, she raised her hand to fend off the next blow. It broke one of her fingers. Six more blows to the head followed, splitting open the scalp to show the shattered skull below. She was now bleeding and unconscious. He bound her wrists, shoved a piece of cloth in her mouth and held the gag in place with strips of yellow insulating tape. Then he raped her.

Angelika then came round and tried to fend him off. He

grabbed a knife and stabbed her 19 times; 16 of the wounds were in her chest and at least 10 were delivered in a frenzy.

He lay her body on some plastic sheeting and a bin-liner they had used to prevent paint splashing on the floor. Earlier, he had discovered a hatch under a rug outside the confessional box. It gave access to the maze of water pipes that ran under the floor. He dragged her there, opened the hatch and dropped her down. Covering her with the plastic sheet, he closed the hatch and replaced the rug. He returned to the garage to clean up. Then he went back to the chapel house to take a shower and get rid of his trousers which were soaked with Angelika's blood.

Martin MacAskill started phoning Angelika's mobile which was now in Tobin's possession. When he got no reply, he became worried.

The following morning, church volunteer Marie Devine arrived to find the shed was still not finished. Tobin complained that his apprentice had not turned up. Then Martin arrived. When he could not find Angelika, he called her sister Aneta who was also in Glasgow. Together, they searched Angelika's room. Nothing was missing, except her mobile phone.

Tobin remained calm throughout this, telling a friend who asked what all the fuss was about, that Martin's girlfriend had gone missing.

Aneta wanted to call the local hospitals; Martin called the police. Two constables arrived an hour later. They searched the premises and took statements from everyone there, including handyman Pat McLaughlin.

Early the following morning, Tobin collected his meagre possessions and left. He lay low in the centre of Glasgow and, that night, took a bus to Edinburgh. Although Father Nugent noticed that his handyman was missing, he knew he had a heart condition that might have been aggravated by Angelika's disappearance.

Everyone joined in the search for Angelika. Meanwhile, the police wanted to interview the missing handyman, thought to be the last person to have seen Angelika, and issued a photograph of him.

In a renewed search of the church and its surrounds, they found a table leg with Angelika's blood on it and several blood-soaked towels. In the bin, they found a pair of jeans with the left knee covered with more of Angelika's blood. It was only that Friday that one of the forensics team stumbled across the hatch in front of the confessional. Opening it, they found her body, still bound and gagged. And in a bin-liner on top of her body, they found a blood-stained kitchen knife.

Back in Paisley, Cheryl McLachlan had seen the handyman's picture on the TV news. She phoned the police and told them that the man they were calling Pat McLaughlin was, in fact, Peter Tobin.

DNA from semen found within Angelika's body matched that from skin fragments found inside the discarded jeans. Fingerprints and palm-prints were found on the plastic sheeting and the bin-liner; more fingerprints were found on the yellow insulation tape wrapped around Angelika's head. They were all from the same person – Peter Tobin – for whom the police had been searching since the attack on Cheryl McLachlan in Paisley. As a registered sex offender, he was also wanted for failing to inform the authorities of his whereabouts.

By then, Tobin was in London and was now calling himself James Kelly. Having previously feigned a heart complaint when in difficulties, he now presented himself at the National Hospital for Neurology and Neurosurgery in Queen Square complaining of chest pains and weakness down the left side. The doctors could find nothing wrong with him and soon suspected that both the symptoms and the name were fictitious.

In the morning, the patient was attended by a male nurse, who stared hard at his face. He returned a few minutes later in a police uniform.

'I knew you were the police,' said Tobin. 'I am relieved you are here.'

'Are you …?' said PC Alan Murray.

'Peter Tobin? Yes. You have been looking for me,' Tobin said.

Later, specks of Angelika's blood were found on his watch. Even so, Tobin pleaded not guilty when he appeared in the High Court in Edinburgh the following March.

During the six-week trial, Tobin denied raping and murdering the young woman and claimed that she had consented to having sex with him. His defence counsel, Donald Findlay QC, drew the jury's attention to Ms Kluk's relationship with former parish priest Father Gerry Nugent and married chauffeur Martin MacAskill. Findlay accused

Father Nugent and witness Matthew Spark-Egan, an alcoholic who had been sitting at the back of the church drinking when Angelika's body was being dragged to its resting place, of being involved in the young woman's death.

Father Nugent was later convicted of contempt of court for his evasive answers during the trial and was forced to resign as a parish priest. He became a drunken recluse and died of a heart attack in 2010.

The jury of eight women and seven men took just under four hours to convict Tobin. The judge, Lord Menzies, described Tobin as 'an evil man' and sentenced him to life, saying he should serve a minimum of 20 years. He told the killer, 'In the course of my time in the law, I have seen many bad men and I have heard evidence about many terrible crimes which have been committed but I have heard no case more tragic, more terrible than this one. The advocate-depute describes what you did to Angelika Kluk as an "atrocity" and that word aptly describes what you did to this young woman.

'Any case of rape is serious; any case of murder is serious. But what you did to Angelika Kluk was inhuman. To bind her hands, gag her so tightly that her face was misshapen when her body was found, to rape her, beat her about the head repeatedly with a table leg fracturing her skull, stab her repeatedly about her chest and body, and then drag her through the church and dump her body under the floorboards as so much rubbish – all this shows utter contempt and disdain for the life of an innocent young woman with her whole life ahead of her.'

After Tobin was found guilty of murdering Angelika Kluk, his third wife Cathy Wilson told the Glasgow-based *Sunday Mail*, 'Some people are saying he should hang, but I don't think so. There shouldn't be a quick fix for him. He should suffer in prison for as long as possible in the worst prison the authorities can put him into. He is truly evil personified.'

The police revealed that, during the investigation, they had found Tobin had used 38 SIM cards in his travels up and down the country. They feared that he might have killed many times before and they began Operation Anagram to re-examine cold cases. Essex Police took a fresh look at the disappearance of Dinah McNicol in 1991, while Strathclyde Police discovered that Vicky Hamilton had disappeared in Bathgate when Tobin had been living there. In all, he was thought to have killed at least 12 women.

Searching Tobin's previous homes yielded a number of pieces of women's jewellery; the fear was that these might be trophies he had kept from his many victims. But the cases of Vicky Hamilton and Dinah McNicol remained top of their list.

When interviewed at Fraserburgh Police Station on 21 July 2007, after Vicky's DNA had been found in his Bathgate home, Tobin denied knowing her and refused to help locate her body.

A new appeal was launched for information concerning Dinah McNicol. Then came a knock on the door of 50 Irvine Drive. Mark Drage, his girlfriend Nicola Downing and her four children, who had lived there peacefully for 12 years, were obliged to move out to a nearby hotel, while their modest three-bedroom terrace house was stripped of its contents.

Two days later, a team of forensic archaeologists scanned the 30-ft back garden with ground-penetrating radar, looking for earth that had been disturbed. It took them just 12 hours before they identified a suspicious patch next to the garden shed. Under a layer of concrete and chalk they found two black plastic bin-liners; one of them had been penetrated by a root. Inside were more bags enclosing a young woman's body that had been cut in two at the waist. She had been bound. The lower half had been buried in a kneeling position, while the upper half had the hands and arms crossed over her face.

Also found in the grave were more lengths of cord, a white bra, a sweatshirt and a red polo shirt. There were also two rings on her fingers that were likely to prove useful in identifying her. Nevertheless, the body was still thought to be that of Dinah McNicol, and her father Ian gave the first reaction to the discovery:

'Considering the short time the investigation has been reopened, I think this development is absolutely fantastic,' he said. 'Hopefully, they will be able to put an end to it, either way ... 99 per cent of me thinks she has been murdered but there's just that 1 per cent that doesn't know. I want to die in peace knowing what happened to my daughter.'

Acting on that 1 per cent, a missing-persons charity

issued a picture of what Dinah might look like if she was still alive at what would be her current age of 34.

The newspapers quickly tied the body in the back garden to Peter Tobin, who was known to have been wanted in connection with at least 12 unsolved murders. Neighbours were shocked. David Martin told the BBC, 'The first thing you realise about Peter Tobin is how normal he is. He's not something that crawls out of the woodwork, even if that's what appears at a later stage. No, he's absolutely normal – like talking to your best mate or someone down the pub.'

Others thought there was something unsettling about him. Former neighbour Laura Harris said she was 'freaked out' by the discovery. 'My mum and dad have lived here for 25 years, but I moved out six years ago,' she said. 'This sort of thing happens to other people. It's awful what has happened and we've lived next door to it for all those years. I remember Tobin … I used to think he was creepy. He wouldn't have been living in the house any longer than two years. He lived there alone, but his son used to visit at weekends. The scary part of it is he offered to babysit me and my sister when we were younger. My mum wasn't having any of it because we didn't know him.'

Although one body had been found, work in the back garden of 50 Irvine Drive did not stop. The soil was shovelled into bags so that it could undergo further forensic testing later. Meanwhile, TV cameras mounted on cherry-pickers (hydraulic cranes with railed platforms, for raising and lowering people) filmed the goings on in the back garden, while one enterprising young lad whose bedroom overlooked the excavation began renting it out to the curious at £10 a time.

The day after the discovery, the officer in charge of the investigation announced that the body the police had found in the back garden probably was not that of Dinah McNicol. The rings and clothes found with her did not match anything Dinah was wearing on the day she went missing. For Dinah's father, it was a setback. 'It's another poor girl,' he said. 'My family hoped it was Dinah so we could finally put her at rest. But it's not finished. They're looking to see if it's another Fred West. They think there might be other bodies there. They thought it might be Dinah because her cash card was used in Margate.'

Over the years, there had been a number of false alarms. 'Any time there comes on the TV or the radio something about a body being found, I think, "Oh my God, no",' Dinah's father said. 'But now I am getting on a bit. I would like to die knowing where she is. For the sake of Dinah and her mother, we would all like a conclusion.'

That afternoon, Lothian and Borders Police confirmed that the body belonged to Vicky Hamilton and they already had a man under arrest. It was clear that the man was Peter Tobin. After he made a brief appearance at Linlithgow Sheriff Court, Vicky's father Michael Hamilton, who had fought to keep the case in the public eye for 16 long years, hammered on the side of the prison van and yelled, 'Die, you bastard!'

His brother Eric issued a statement that read: 'All I can

say is that Mike is happy the long road is nearly at an end. We just want peace and to put Vicky where she belongs.'

Later that day, the police announced that they had found a second body. This time, the jewellery and clothing did match those of Dinah McNicol and the identity of the corpse was confirmed by dental records and DNA profiling soon after. Although the horrific circumstances of her death were also revealed, Ian McNicol responded to the news with dignity: 'The 1 per cent has gone now ... we can actually have her remains, put her remains next to her mother's, actually have time to mourn and get on with life.'

Since the disappearance of Dinah, he had been trying to shield the other two young children he had been bringing up single-handed. At one time, he feared she may have been a victim of Fred West.

When Tobin went on trial for the murder of Vicky Hamilton in November 2008, he claimed to have been in the Portsmouth area when she disappeared, but witnesses reported seeing him Bathgate. After four weeks of evidence, it took the jury of nine women and three men less than two-and-a-half hours to find him guilty.

Sentencing him to life with a tariff of at least 30 years, the judge said, 'This was a vulnerable teenager who needed help on her way home, but instead she fell into your clutches and you brought her short life to an end in a disgusting and degrading way. No one will ever know what fear and torment Vicky Hamilton went through before she died. But the agony you caused to her family was made infinitely worse by your calculating and entirely self-interested attempts to conceal and avoid detection for what you had done. After a lengthy trial in which you conceded nothing, you have now been convicted as a result of your own mistakes ... Abducting and killing a child on her way home from a happy weekend with her sister and then desecrating her body must rank among the most evil and horrific acts that any human being could commit.'

Vicky's sister said, 'We are glad this 17-year nightmare has finally come to an end. There were many times when we thought this day wouldn't come. We are hoping we can now move on as a family and start to remember Vicky as the loving sister she was before she was so tragically and cruelly taken from us. Vicky's abduction also robbed us of our mum, Janette, who never came to terms with the fact Vicky never came home that night and who died of a broken heart two years later, never knowing what happened to her daughter. We take comfort in the knowledge that Mum and Vicky have been looking over us and giving us the strength needed to cope during these difficult times.'

At his trial for the murder of Dinah McNicol in December 2009, Tobin instructed his counsel not to offer any defence. However, he pleaded not guilty, so the prosecution had to take the time and trouble to prove its case. Given the evidence, this was not too difficult. On the first day of the trial, the jury were told that Tobin was a convicted paedophile who had already been sentenced to life for the murder of Vicky Hamilton, whose body had been found next to Dinah's in Tobin's back garden.

In his closing statement, the prosecutor, William Clegg QC, told the jury, 'Did a stranger arrive at 50 Irvine Drive to find that the occupier had conveniently dug a hole and then dumped her body in it? And of all the gardens in the south-east of England, the murderer of Dinah McNicol happens to select the garden of another murderer who had already buried his victim there? If this were not so serious, it would be ludicrous.'

The jury took just 13 minutes to deliver a unanimous verdict of guilty. The judge, Mr Justice Calvert-Smith, told Tobin, 'This is the third time you have stood in the dock for murder. On all three occasions, the evidence against you was overwhelming. Yet even now you refuse to come to terms with your guilt.' Handing down a third life sentence, the judge said he should never be released.

Ian McNicol was in court to hear the verdict and showed no emotion. He was joined in the public gallery by Michael Hamilton.

Outside the court, Dinah's half-sister Sara Tizard said, 'After all these years, we at last know the truth and justice has prevailed. We would like to put the trial behind us and remember Dinah as the unique and inspiring daughter and sister that she was.'

DS Tim Wills of Essex Police, who oversaw the investigation in the back garden, said, 'Peter Tobin I can only describe as pure evil. He has shown no remorse for killing Dinah or any of the other women he has been convicted of killing.'

DS David Swindle of Strathclyde Police, who set up

Operation Anagram, said, 'Peter Tobin has now been found guilty for the brutal murders of three young women. Who knows if he has killed others? No stone will be left unturned and every single piece of information gathered will be investigated by forces throughout the UK to establish if he was responsible for any other crimes.'

When he was convicted of the murder of Vicky Hamilton, Tobin boasted to a prison psychiatrist that he had killed 48 women, then taunted, 'Prove it.'

What had driven Tobin to such hatred of women is not clear. There has been speculation that the menstrual cycle somehow angered him. This was also true of 'Bible John', the nickname given to the serial killer who murdered three women in Glasgow in the 1960s. He has never been caught or identified and, as late as December 2004, the Scottish police were still actively investigating the case, as many experts on serial killing believe that Bible John and Peter Tobin are one and the same.

Bible John's first victim was 25-year-old nurse Patricia Docker. On the evening of 22 February 1968, she decided that she needed a night out. Her husband, a corporal in the RAF, was stationed in England, and she was staying with her parents with her young son. It was a Thursday night and they were happy to babysit.

She got dressed up for the occasion and fixed her hair. It seems she went to a number of ballrooms that evening. She was seen at the Majestic Ballroom in Hope Street, then moved on to Barrowland Ballroom in Gallowgate (often referred to as 'The Barrowland'). This was popular with her friends as, on a Thursday night, it catered to those aged 25 and over. It was busy and Patricia did not particularly stand out, and it was difficult to identify all her dance partners. However, it seems that someone offered to walk her home. She never got there.

At dawn the following morning, a cabinet maker on his way to work found the naked body of a dead woman in a quiet lane behind Carmichael Place, a few yards from Patricia's parents' house in Langside Place. She had been strangled with her own tights. None of her other clothing could be found. The police determined that she had been dead for several hours and they came to believe that she had been strangled elsewhere and dumped there. When Patricia Docker did not return home, the police came to the obvious conclusion and Patricia's parents had the terrible task of identifying the body.

The police widened their search for her clothes, handbag and other belongings. Divers even searched the river nearby, but nothing was found. One local resident told the police that she thought she had heard cries for help during the early hours of 23 February, but none of the journalists or photographers who had attended a colleague's party near where the body was found that night remember anything. A photograph of a policewoman dressed in clothes similar to those Patricia was wearing that night was circulated in the area, but no one remembered seeing her after she left the dance hall.

Glasgow had had recent experience of serial killers. Ian Brady, convicted of the Moors Murders in 1966, had been born there. Ten years before Patricia Docker was killed, Peter Manuel had been hanged. A sociopath and burglar, he had killed at least eight people. So when Patricia's naked body was found dumped in the street, Glaswegians feared the worst. But that did not stop them having fun.

A year-and-a-half later, 32-year-old Jemima McDonald fancied a Saturday night out. On the evening of 16 August 1969, she dropped off her three kids with her sister Margaret for the night, then headed for The Barrowland. High bouffant hairstyles were still in fashion in Glasgow in 1969 and she travelled across town with a scarf over her hair. When she arrived at the ballroom, she went into the Ladies (toilet) where she took out her rollers and finished off her make-up.

On the dance floor, Jemima attracted attention. Other dancers noticed that she spent much of the evening dancing with a tall man in his late twenties or early thirties. He wore a blue suit and was tall and slim; his red hair was cut short and his appearance was neat. And early the next morning, she was seen leaving the ballroom with him.

The next day, Jemima did not come to pick up her kids as expected. Margaret grew worried. Later that day, she overheard street children talking about a body they had discovered in a derelict building in MacKeith Street nearby. Fearing the worst, Margaret got the kids to direct her to the building. There she found her sister's battered body.

Jemima was fully clothed, but there were similarities to the Patricia Docker case: both women had been strangled with their own pantyhose; both had been found near their home. Jemima's handbag was missing and screams had been heard that night. Later, the police found another similarity between the two cases – both had been having their period when they were killed.

A search of the area rendered no new clues and an attempt to question those who had been at The Barrowland that night also proved fruitless, as many of them were married and were out with people who were not their spouses. An appeal from the dance hall's stage also drew a blank. A policewoman dressed in Jemima's clothes retraced her final steps. The police released a sketch of the tall man she had been seen with when she was leaving The Barrowland and, for the first time in a Scottish murder investigation, Jemima's family offered a reward of £100. Everything proved futile.

Despite all the publicity the murders were getting, it did not put people off going to The Barrowland. Twenty-nine-year-old Helen Puttock was hell-bent on going there on the night of 30 October 1969. Her husband, a soldier, who was going to stay at home with their two young boys, begged his wife to be careful. But Helen was not worried; she would not be alone. She was going with her sister Jean and was sure they would be safe together.

At The Barrowland, they met two young men, both called John. One said he came from Castlemilk. Helen spent most of the evening dancing with the other John. He was tall, slim and had red hair. When they left The Barrowland, Castlemilk John shared the two sisters' taxi. During the journey, the man said that his name was John, he played golf badly, but a cousin had recently hit a hole-in-one. Jean also remembered he mentioned that he had a sister; he said that they had been raised in a strict religious household and he was still able to quote long passages of the Bible – hence his nickname. The surname he gave, Jean recalled, was Templeton, Emerson or Sempleson. Tobin was a Roman Catholic with a strong religious background; as we have seen, he regularly used pseudonyms. One of them was John Semple.

He spoke of how his father regarded dance halls, such as The Barrowland, as 'dens of iniquity', condemning the women who frequented them as evil. He also referred to Moses and said, 'I don't drink at Hogmanay. I pray.'

Bible John also seemed upset by Jean's presence; he wanted be alone with Helen. Ignoring Jean for much of the ride, he did not even say goodbye when they dropped her off.

The next morning, Helen's fully clothed body was found in the street by a man walking his dog. Again, she had been strangled with her own nylons and her handbag was missing. She, too, was menstruating when she was murdered. As if to draw attention to the fact, the killer had removed her sanitary towel and tucked it under her armpit. And this time he had left two clues that might help identify him – a semen stain on her tights and a bite mark on her wrist.

Thanks to Jean, the police now had an accurate description of the man they wanted to question. The suspect was around 6ft tall, and of medium build. He had blue-grey eyes and light reddish hair, which he kept cut short. His watch had a military-style band. The teeth marks on the body showed that two teeth in the upper-right part of the mouth overlapped.

A new artist's impression of the suspect was circulated – this one in colour. It prompted over 4,000 calls from people who thought they had seen or knew the man in the picture. Jean was called to the police station over 250 times to see suspects, but none of them turned out to be the man she and her sister had shared a taxi with. Men who bore a resemblance to the killer but had been eliminated from the inquiry were issued with cards by the police showing they had been questioned and cleared. One of them was used in a reconstruction of Helen's last evening, with a police-woman playing her part that was aired on BBC television. Helen's husband made an appeal to his wife's killer to turn himself in, and offered his life savings as a reward for information leading to his arrest.

Over 50,000 statements were taken and over 100 policemen worked on the case. Younger officers in plain clothes mingled with the dancers in The Barrowland. Taxi drivers and bus crews received particular attention. One man said he had seen a young male with scratches on his face on the bus on 31 October. He had got off at a stop on Gray Street. Police combed the area, but found nothing.

The suspect's military wristwatch band and his short hair led the police to believe that he might be a member of the armed forces – or even a policeman. Dentists were questioned about patients with overlapping teeth, and staff at nearby golf clubs were asked about anyone who had recently scored a hole-in-one. A Dutch psychic called in by a local newspaper was inspired to draw a map, but a search of the area drew a blank.

Since it was the mid-1970s psychological profiling had yet to be developed, however a Glasgow psychiatrist said that although Bible John was sociable, he was prudish. He would probably read widely on subjects ranging from sorcery to the Nazis and go to the cinema by himself. This did not help.

Although only three murders have been officially ascribed to Bible John, he may have committed others. In 1977, another young woman who spent her last night in a Glasgow dance hall was found strangled and without her handbag. This sparked a new round of interest in Bible John. In 1983, a wealthy Glasgow man hired a private detective to find a childhood friend whom he thought resembled Bible John. The man was found living in the Netherlands and was cleared.

Another man who had been cleared was John McInnes, a suspect in the investigation in the 1960s. He bore a close resemblance to the sketch of the suspect, but Jean had failed to identify him. Nevertheless, he continued to be a prime suspect until, in 1981, he committed suicide.

In the 1960s, DNA fingerprinting was as yet undreamt of. But in 1996, DNA from the semen left on Helen Puttock's tights was compared to a sample taken from one of John McInnes's siblings. The match was inconclusive; nevertheless the police requested the exhumation of

John McInnes's body from a graveyard in Stonehouse, Lanarkshire.

The resulting publicity led to the harassment of McInnes's family. But when the tests were completed it was found that his DNA did not match that in the semen on Helen Puttock's tights; neither did his teeth match the bite-mark on her wrist. Jean said that she always knew that McInnes was not the killer and she had repeatedly told Strathclyde Police they had the wrong man. John McInnes was re-buried and finally left to rest in peace.

But the investigation was still not over. In October 2000, Professor Ian Stephen, a leading criminal psychologist who is said to have inspired TV's *Cracker*, passed the name of a new suspect on to the Lothian and Borders Police, asking them to forward it to Strathclyde. He said he had obtained the new lead from an expatriate Scot living in the USA who suspected that a member of his extended family was Bible John. The suspect was the son of a policeman; he had been married in the Glasgow area and lived in Lanarkshire with his wife and two children, until he moved to England in 1970.

According to the file Professor Stephen passed to the police, the suspect's behaviour changed dramatically in the late 1960s, when he increasingly went out alone at night and sometimes failed to return until the following day.

Professor Stephen told the BBC, 'I would like to think that his name has already been considered and ruled out but I am not hopeful. The police were looking for a stereotype, a known sex offender at the time. The profile appears to fit that of Bible John. While the information is circumstantial, I think the police have got to have a serious look at it.'

The Strathclyde Police said they would look at the new information.

In December 2004, DNA taken from a Glasgow crime scene two years earlier was an 80 per cent match to the semen found on Helen's tights. Samples were still being collected from a number of suspects in their fifties and sixties and, in May 2005, a spokesman for the police said, 'Science will solve these killings. We have no doubt of that.'

That October, Strathclyde Police set up a new Unresolved Case Unit to re-examine the evidence in the Bible John Killings.

Dr Adrian Linacre, a lecturer in forensic science at Strathclyde University, said new processes could be employed to identify traces of evidence which previously could not be found. 'Now with the advent of DNA profiling, someone who's just held something for a brief period, or held someone, you're going to transfer your DNA,' he said.

However, Joe Jackson, a detective involved the Bible John investigation who went on to become head of Glasgow's CID, dismissed the DNA evidence. As DNA fingerprinting was not developed until 1984, he said it was unlikely that the samples from the 1960s had been collected or stored properly. 'Bloodstained clothing used to be stored in plastic bags,' he said. 'Scientists told us to dry them out and put them in plastic bags, which caused them to ferment eventually. The drying-out process usually involved the items being draped over pipes in the boiler room of police offices. I cannot say for certain how the tights were stored, but I cannot see them being treated as gingerly as would be necessary for a clear DNA comparison.'

It also had to be remembered that the semen stain on her tights may not necessarily have come from the killer.

Jackson also commented on the unconventional policing methods used in the Bible John investigation. 'I formed part of what the press called the Marine Formation Dance team – detectives assigned to attend dance halls,' he said. 'We'd dance with customers and question them while showing nifty footwork. It was a dirty job but someone had to do it.'

Joe Jackson is convinced that Bible John is Tobin. 'I saw his photo after the church killing and thought, "This is as near Bible John as you're going to get",' he said.

Tobin was in his early twenties, and living in Glasgow at the time of the Bible John killings, and he was a regular at city dance halls. He met his first wife, Margaret Mackintosh, then 17, at a Glasgow dance hall in 1968. Soon he was raping, beating and strangling her, driven to violence by her menstrual cycle. Tobin left Scotland in 1969, the year the killings stopped.

After Tobin's conviction, detectives issued pictures of him as a younger man, and these do bear a striking similarity to the artist's impression of Bible John drawn up at the time. DS David Swindle, head of Operation Anagram, said, 'The picture might jog people's memories. Everything indicates that Tobin has probably killed other people.'

When the picture of the young Tobin was shown on *Crimewatch* in 2010, 63-year-old Julia Taylor came forward. She said that he had approached her in The Barrowland dance hall 40 years before and had pestered her to go to a party in Castlemilk with him. 'I couldn't believe my eyes when I saw the pictures of Tobin as a young man,' she said. 'It was the man who came up to me so many years ago in The Barrowland. I am 100 per cent certain Tobin is Bible John.'

She often went to go dancing at The Barrowland with her friends in the late 1960s, despite the Bible John scare. 'There was one night that I have never forgotten, when this weird man asked me to dance,' she told the *Daily Record*. 'I got separated from my pals and he came up to me – there was something odd, cold and clinical about him. He seemed to be always thinking and wasn't that warm and friendly, although he was extremely polite.' She had never forgotten him. 'He wore a silver-grey suit which was very well cut and a blue shirt with a plain, coloured tie. He looked a bit out of place as he was so over-dressed. He did not want to dance on the main floor and took me to the upstairs dance floor. It was quieter there. He kept asking me to go to a party in Castlemilk and was extremely persistent but I told him that I didn't know him or the area.'

At the time, because of the Bible John panic, there were posters warning women to be careful. 'When I kept refusing to go to the party, his whole face and attitude changed,' she said. 'He turned from being charming to being really odd and frightening. He said, "You better get off the dance floor because I am not dancing with you any more."'

Julia remembered walking off the floor to get her coat as the man circled around watching her. 'It was chilling,' she said. 'I saw a bouncer and I was going to tell him to check the man out but I was scared. I just ran out and never stopped. I looked back and he was watching me, glaring at me. I was scared stiff and I have never forgotten that feeling of total terror.'

Tobin's first wife Margaret Mackintosh remembered visiting his parents in Paisley, just a few miles outside Glasgow. Before they were married, he took her to Earlbank Avenue, 200 yards from where Helen Puttock was found. She also remarked that he enjoyed having sex with her when she was menstruating. The sight of blood turned him on.

Back then, Tobin dressed like Bible John, in a conservative suit. Under normal circumstances both of these killers were polite, even chivalrous. Both Tobin and Bible John sexually assaulted and strangled their victims, using their clothing as gags or ligatures. Gang violence was prevalent in Glasgow at the time of the Bible John killings. He would have been searched on his way into a dance hall, so he would not have been able to carry a knife.

Professor David Wilson, an expert on serial killers, points out that Bible John was not the type of murderer who would quit while he was still at large, and Tobin was uncharacteristically old to have started killing at the age of 44, if Vicky Hamilton was his first victim.

Among the collection of women's jewellery found in Tobin's former home was a cap badge from the Royal

Electrical and Mechanical Engineers, the regiment Helen Puttock's husband belonged to.

There are other murders that Tobin is thought to have been responsible for. He was a regular visitor to the Norfolk coast and, as part of Operation Anagram, the Norfolk Constabulary began to re-examine the case of April Fabb who had disappeared on 8 April 1969. The 13-year-old was cycling the mile-and-a-half from Metton, near Cromer, to Roughton to deliver a packet of cigarettes to her brother-in-law. Her blue-and-white bicycle was found by the side of the road, but she was nowhere to be seen. It is thought that Tobin was in the area at the time. In 2010, a well nearby was excavated but it did not produce any fresh leads.

Eighteen-year-old Jackie Ansell Lamb was hitchhiking from London to Manchester on 8 March 1970 when she went missing. A woman answering her description was seen getting into a car at Keele Services between 4.00pm and 5.00pm. A farmer found her body in a wood near Knutsford, Cheshire, six days later. She had been sexually assaulted and strangled. Tobin used the M1 on his numerous trips between Scotland and southern England.

On 10 March 1970, 18-year-old insurance clerk Susan Long disappeared after leaving the Gala Ballroom in Norwich and heading home to Aylsham nine miles away. On the way, she was raped and strangled. Her body was found the next morning in a lovers' lane dumped in the street near her home, like the victims of Bible John.

In October 1970, 24-year-old teacher Barbara Mayo went missing after leaving her home in London to go hitch-hiking. Her half-naked body was found six days later by walkers in a wood at Hardwick Hall, a National Trust stately home near Chesterfield, Derbyshire, less than a mile from the M1. She had been raped, punched around the head and strangled with a length of flex.

During Operation Anagram, the Norwich police also reinvestigated the case of a headless woman's body found at the side of the road in Cockley Cley, near Swaffham, in 1974. She was wearing a frilly, pink Marks and Spencer's nightdress and was bound in a way similar to Dinah McNicol. The body was wrapped in brown plastic sheeting bearing the initials 'NCR'. The Scottish company National Cash Register only made six sheets of this between 1962 and 1968; Tobin had been in Glasgow at the time. He had also used plastic sheeting to wrap the bodies of Vicky Hamilton and Angelika Kluk. The police even disinterred the headless woman's body but no further connection to Tobin could be established.

A few days after the discovery of the headless corpse, 21-year-old Pamela Exall went missing from the Dinglea Campsite in Snettisham, 20 miles from Cockley Cley.

Thirteen-year-old Genette Tate, fourteen-year-old Susanne Lawrence and twenty-two-year-old Jessie Earl were all killed in a two-year period from 1978–80 after Tobin's second marriage broke up. Genette had been abducted from her paper round. As in the case of April Fabb, her bicycle was found but no trace of her body has ever come to light. Her father said she bore a striking resemblance to Dinah McNicol.

Less than a year later, in July 1979, Suzanne Lawrence left her sister's home in Harold Hill to make her way home to nearby Romford. She never arrived. On his journeys between the south coast and Norfolk, Tobin would have travelled through Harold Hill.

Art student Jessie Earl went missing from her bedsit in Eastbourne in 1980. Her body was found on Beachy Head nine years later. Her wrists had been tied with her bra, as Vicky Hamilton's had been. During Operation Anagram, the police visited her parents' home to see if they could collect some DNA evidence that might link her to Tobin, who was living just 25 miles away in Brighton when she went missing. He moved back to Glasgow soon afterwards. After his known killings, he regularly put some distance between him and the scenes of the crimes.

Fourteen-year-old Patsy Morris disappeared in London in 1980. Her body was discovered hidden in undergrowth on Hounslow Heath in mid-summer. Her father, George Morris, believes that she might have been one of Tobin's victims. 'As soon as I read about the other girl's body being found in his backyard, something inside me clicked,' he said.

In 1981, the body of 16-year-old Pamela Hastie was found in Rannoch Woods in Johnstone, Renfrewshire, the town where Tobin had been born. She had been raped and strangled. A local man served 21 years for her murder, but the case against him was quashed in 2007 and the police began investigating Tobin for the offence. Ten years earlier, the naked body of 37-year-old mother-of-two, Dorothea

Meechan, had been found in Renfrew. Her clothes and handbag were missing and beside the body was a note that said, 'Mr Polis, I have killed that woman in cold blood. Bible John.' Richard 'The Snake' Coubrough spent 34 years in jail for strangling her. He was freed in 2005, but the case was still in front of the Court of Criminal Appeal when he died. The police also investigated Tobin for the murder.

The bodies of nine-year-old Nicola Fellows and her playmate, ten-year-old Karen Hadaway, were found in Wild Park on the outskirts of Brighton in October 1986. Both had been raped and strangled. Twenty-year-old Russell Bishop was charged, and a jury eventually took just two hours to find him not guilty. Tobin was living in Brighton at the time.

In 1988, 18-year-old Louise Kay had been out clubbing in Eastbourne on the night she disappeared. She drove a girlfriend home in her dad's Ford Fiesta, dropping her off at 4.30am. She said she intended to drive back to her parents' house, which was just outside the town. However, neither Louise nor the car have been seen since. Tobin was working in a hotel in Eastbourne at the time of her disappearance.

The half-naked body of 16-year-old prostitute Natalie Pearman was found at Ringland Hills, near Norwich, in November 1992. She was found strangled after disappearing from the red-light district of Norwich. The case was briefly linked to Steve Wright, who was convicted of the murder of five prostitutes in Ipswich in 2006. Her killer has never been found. Again, Tobin frequented the area.

On 23 December 1992, 14-year-old Johanna Young left

home to go to the local fish-and-chip shop in Watton. Her semi-naked body was found on Boxing Day in a waterlogged pit near Wayland Wood, just eight miles from where the headless woman had been found in 1974. She had a fractured skull, but had still been alive when her assailant dumped her and she drowned.

When Sussex Police heard of Tobin's frenzied knife attack on Angelika Kluk in 2006, they began investigating any connection he might have had to the death of 35-year-old mother-of-three Jennifer Kiely, who had been stabbed 16 times. Her body was found in a beach shelter in Eastbourne where the killer had tried to burn it.

While the police have not been able to establish that Tobin was responsible for any of these murders – and he is not saying – Profession Wilson and Joe Jackson remain convinced that he was Bible John.

8

A HEAD IN THE FLOWER BED

Ed Kemper is one of a number of American murderers who have earned the sobriquet 'The Co-Ed Killer'. After killing his grandparents when he was just 15, he went on to kill and dismember six female hitch-hikers in the Santa Cruz area of California. His usual method of disposal was to dump their remains in remote rural areas, but he buried the head of 19-year-old Cindy Schall in his mother's back garden, joking that his mother 'always wanted people to look up to her'. Later, he killed his mother, too, along with one of her friends, then turned himself in to the authorities.

Edmund Emil Kemper III was born in Burbank, California, on 18 December 1948. He was the second child of Edmund Emil Kemper Jr and his wife Clarnell. He had two sisters – Susan was six years older than him and Allyn two years younger. Both his parents were big. His father was 6ft 8in tall and his mother was over 6ft. Ed grew up to be a giant – 6ft 9in tall, and weighing over 20 stone.

Dad worked as an electrician, but he had been a hero in the Second World War, serving in a special forces unit in Europe. He loved to collect guns and other weapons, and Ed hero-worshipped him.

Ed's parents did not get on. After a series of heated arguments and trial separations, they split for good in 1957. Clarnell and the children went to live in Montana, where she worked in a bank. But Ed missed his dad and became emotional and clingy. Fearing he might become a homosexual, his mother tried toughening him up by putting him to bed in the basement with a heavy table over the trapdoor, the only way out. This continued for eight months, until his father came by for a visit and put a stop to it, but things barely improved. He complained that his mother was 'an alcoholic and constantly bitched and screamed at me'.

When he was just nine, he buried the family's cat alive in the back garden. The reason was, he later said, because it had transferred its affections to his two sisters and he had killed it 'to make it mine'. It was the beginning of a grisly career. Later, he dug it up, cut off its head and stuck it on the end of a stick. He kept this gruesome relic in his bedroom and prayed to it. A year later, on a visit to New York, he tried to jump off the top of the Empire State Building, but was restrained by an aunt.

Already he was having fantasies about murdering people – sometimes all together, otherwise one at a time.

His fantasy victims were mostly women and he dreamt of carrying their bodies off as trophies that he could love and cherish.

His little sister Allyn was upset at his habit of cutting up her dolls. In school, he was an outcast. He would annoy the other kids by sitting and staring at them. Although he was a big child, he was branded a weakling and a coward, and excluded from their games.

He was alienated further in 1961 when his father remarried, acquiring a stepson who was two years older; his mother also remarried the following year. Soon after, Ed was accused of shooting a classmate's dog, further enhancing his status as a pariah. Then he killed the family's new cat with a machete because he thought it was ignoring him.

Plainly, Ed was disturbed and his mother sent him back to southern California to live with his father. But his stepmother found his brooding silences and icy stare unsettling so, at Christmas, his father took Ed to live with his own parents on their isolated farm at North Fork, high in California's Sierra Mountains. It was not a good move.

His grandparents were well meaning. Grandpaps Edmund gave Ed a rifle to shoot rabbits and gophers on the ranch, but he was dull company and perhaps a little senile. Grandma Maud wrote and illustrated children's books, but she reminded him of his mother, always bossing him about. She did not seem to trust him and always reminded him that he should be grateful that they were looking after him.

'My grandmother thought she had more balls than any man and was constantly emasculating me and my grandfather to prove it,' said Kemper. 'I couldn't please her. It was like being in jail. I became a walking time bomb and I finally blew. It was like that the second time, with my mother.'

Kemper remembered one incident when his grandmother went on a shopping trip to Fresno, leaving him at home alone. She had her husband's .45 automatic with her in her purse because she was afraid Ed might play around with it in her absence.

'I saw her big black pocketbook bulging as she went out the door and I said to myself, "Why, that old bitch, she's taking the gun with her, because she doesn't trust me, even though I promised I wouldn't touch it,"' he later recalled.

He said he looked in his grandfather's bureau drawer and, he said, 'Sure enough, the gun was gone from its usual place. I toyed with the idea of calling the chief of police in Fresno and telling him, "There's a little old lady walking around town with a .45 in her purse and she's planning a hold-up ..." and then give him my grandmother's description. How do you suppose she would have talked herself out of that?'

When Ed was 15, he went to visit his mother in Montana, returning to his grandparent's ranch early in August. Soon afterwards, he was sitting in the kitchen with his grandmother, who was checking the proofs of her latest book. His icy stare made her tetchy, so he took his gun to go out and shoot something. She called after him, telling him not to shoot any birds. Ed turned and shot her twice in the back of the head.

He was dragging her body into the bedroom when he

heard his grandfather's car pulling up outside. The old man had been into town to buy groceries. Ed watched as he got out of the car. He brought the rifle to his shoulder, took aim and killed him with a single shot. He put the old man's body in the garage and hosed down the yard.

It was only then that he realised he was in trouble, so he phoned his mother and asked her what to do. She told him to phone the local sheriff. He did what he was told, telling the officer he had killed the old lady because 'I just wondered how it would feel to shoot Grandma'. He had then shot his grandfather so that he would never have to know that his wife was dead. Besides, he might have been angry with him.

Diagnosed as a paranoid schizophrenic, Kemper did not have to stand trial and, on 6 December 1964, just a few days shy of his 16th birthday, he was sent to the Atascadero State Hospital, a secure facility for the criminally insane. Strictly speaking, he should not have been there; the hospital was for adults. But there was nowhere else to put him. Nevertheless, he got on well there. By nature, he was quiet and peaceable. He was also highly intelligent and became a member of the Junior Chamber of Commerce there. Later, at his trial, he wore his pin with pride. And, by the age of 19, he had worked his way up to being head of the psychological testing lab.

Working directly under the hospital's chief psychologist, he picked up the language and theory of psychology, even – ironically – helping develop the 'Overt Hostility Scale'. But that was not all he learned. Atascadero specialised in treating sex offenders and Kemper went to group therapy sessions with rapists. They had all been caught because their victims had informed on them. It was better, he figured, not to leave the victims alive.

Ed had never thought there was anything wrong with him. But having learned the ins and outs of the system, he realised that it was best that he convinced the doctors he had been ill, but was better now. It worked. After four years, the psychologists at the hospital thought that he was well on the way to be cured, provided he stayed away from his mother who, they believed, had a borderline personality disorder.

Kemper was 20 when he was released into a halfway house. Although he had been out of circulation for less than five years, the world around him had changed radically. He was still steeped in the Second World War values of his father and the conservative ethos of law and order. Now people his age were taking on the police in civil rights and anti-war demonstrations.

'When I got out on the street, it was like being on a strange planet,' he said. 'People my age were not talking the same language. I had been living with people older than I was for so long that I was an old fogey.' Particular contempt was reserved for hippies. They were seen as low class and immoral, particularly the long-haired young girls he saw hitching rides with strangers.

He complained that he did not get help from any parole officer to support his reintegration into society. Instead, after three months in the halfway house and against the advice of the psychologists, he was released into the custody of his mother. She was now working as an administrative assistant at the University of California at Santa Cruz and he went to live with her in the nearby town of Aptos. They did not get on any better than they had before. She was, he said, a 'big, ugly, awkward woman who was 6ft tall and she was always trying to get me to go out with girls who were just like her ... friends of hers from the campus.' He preferred petite girls.

Kemper thought that she was a vindictive, argumentative harridan. This was not how her colleagues saw her. At the university she was well liked, but Kemper complained she had a divided personality. 'She was Mrs Wonderful up on the campus, had everything under control,' he said. 'When she comes home, she lets everything down and she's just a pure bitch; busts her butt being super nice at work and comes home at night and is a shit.'

He resented the way she had thrown out his father, whom he idolised. Since then, she had remarried and divorced twice more.

His relationship with his father was little better. 'He didn't want me around, because I upset his second wife,' said Kemper. 'Before I went to Atascadero, my presence gave her migraine headaches; when I came out, she was going to have a heart attack if I came around.'

At least his mother was prepared to take him in, despite everything. 'She loved me in her way and, despite all the violent screaming and yelling arguments we had, I loved her, too,' he said. 'But she had to manage your life ... and interfere in your personal affairs.'

She wanted her son to go to college and get a degree. He preferred to hang out at local bars, particularly one called the Jury Room which was frequented by off-duty cops. He applied to join the force, but was rejected because of his size. He was just too big.

Instead, he got a job manning a stop-go sign for a state road-works gang. With his wages, he bought a motorbike, but soon crashed it, injuring his head. With the insurance payout, he bought a 1969 two-door sedan, a Ford Galaxie.

Now he was earning money, he moved out from his mother's house and shared a rented flat with a friend in Alameda, near San Francisco. In his spare time, he cruised the California highways, picking up female hitch-hikers and learning to make himself pleasant and agreeable.

'At first, I picked up girls just to talk to them, just to try to get acquainted with people my own age and try to strike up a friendship,' he said. Then he began to have sex fantasies about the girls he picked up hitchhiking, but feared being caught and convicted as a rapist. The bloodlust he had since childhood provided the solution. 'I decided to mix the two,' he said, 'and have a situation of rape and murder and no witnesses and no prosecution.'

He went about his campaign of sexual assault and homicide methodically. Knowing that he was most likely to be spotted when he was picking up the girls, he tried to make himself as inconspicuous as possible, despite his size. He learned to spot potential victims a long way off so that he did not have to turn back or make any manoeuvres that drew attention to his car.

Once he had satisfied his lust and murdered the victim, he would dispose of the body in a remote place, hundreds of miles from where he was living. His work on the road gang introduced him to some of the wilder parts of the state and the wilderness techniques he had learned as a Boy Scout would help him conceal the bodies.

He already knew that there were more hitch-hikers on the roads at weekends and that young women were more likely to get into his car when it was raining. He also decided that he would never go out when excited or angry. It was key that his crimes were well planned and committed when he was in control. And he resolved not to keep anything – a weapon or any of the victims' personal possessions – that might tie him to the crime. Before long, he broke every one of these rules but the police still had no clue to his identity until he gave himself up.

He started buying knives and borrowed a 9mm Browning automatic pistol from a friend. It was now time to put his plans into action.

Kemper's first two victims were 18-year-old Fresno State college co-eds, Mary Ann Pesce and Anita Luchessa, whom he picked up in Berkeley. 'I had full intentions of killing them,' he said.

On the afternoon of 7 May 1972, the two girls were hitch-hiking to visit friends in Stanford University, no more than an hour's drive away. The pair got in the back seat and Kemper struck up a conversation. It did not take long for him to figure out that they did not know where they were going. Instead of driving south towards

Stanford, he headed inland on the freeways, then pulled off onto a side road.

When the girls asked him what he was doing, he pulled the borrowed pistol from under the seat. He said that they were going back to his apartment. One of them would have to ride in the front seat with him, where he could keep an eye on her. The other would have to get in the trunk.

He pulled a pair of handcuffs from under the driver's seat and cuffed Mary Ann's hands behind her back. Anita was then taken to the trunk at gunpoint.

But he was not taking them back to his apartment. In the front seat, he put a plastic bag over Mary Ann's head and wound a cord around her neck. Fighting for her life, she bit through the bag and managed to catch the cord in her mouth. Killing her was not as easy as he thought it would be.

He pulled out a knife and began stabbing her. She did her best to dodge the blows, all the time pleading for her life. But Kemper just grabbed hold of her face and slit her throat.

Then he went round to the trunk, opened it and told the terrified girl that he had hit Mary Ann because she had struggled and he needed her help. As Anita climbed out of the trunk, he lunged at her with another knife. He kept stabbing until she fell back dead into the trunk. Then he tossed the knife in after her and closed the boot.

He was unapologetic and only regretted that it was all over so quickly. 'I would loved to have raped them, but not having any experience at all ...' he said.

He drove back to his apartment in Alameda. His flatmate was out. Wrapping the two girls' bodies in blankets, he carried them up to his room where he began dismembering them, taking Polaroid photographs of their naked bodies and the grisly process of cutting them up. Curiously, he confessed to having feelings of tenderness towards Mary Ann Pesce, even as he butchered her. 'I was really quite struck by her personality and her looks and there was just almost a reverence there,' he said.

He had oral sex with her severed head. Then he destroyed the girls' meagre possessions and carried them and the body parts back out to the car. Anita Luchessa's remains were thrown out into the brush on a hillside. Mary Ann Pesce's body parts were buried in a redwood grove on a mountain highway. He kept their decapitated heads for some time, then threw them down a ravine on one of his forays into the hills.

Again, for Kemper, Mary Ann Pesce was special and he returned to the redwood grove. 'Sometimes, afterward, I visited there … to be near her … because I loved her and wanted her,' he said. After his arrest, he took investigators to the grave where he had buried her.

Meanwhile, the girls went on California's burgeoning missing-persons list until, months later, Mary Ann Pesce's head was found by hikers and she was identified from dental records. But the trail of the killer had gone cold. Neither Anita Luchessa's head nor her body were ever found.

For the time being, Kemper's lust for killing was satisfied.

He had the girls' addresses from the contents of their handbags and liked to drive past their houses, imagining the grief felt by their families within.

In a motorcycle accident, he fractured his arm and had to have a metal plate inserted. During his enforced lay-off from work, he spent his time getting his juvenile record deleted. Having to admit to murder on application forms made it difficult to get jobs and impossible to buy a gun.

On 14 September 1972, 15-year-old Aiko Koo was waiting for the bus in University Avenue in Berkeley. She was tiny and slender, a talented dancer in both ballet and classical Korean styles. Fearing that she might be late for her dance class in San Francisco she accepted a lift from a seemingly helpful stranger. A witness said the driver who picked her up was a tall Caucasian male with light or medium brown hair driving a cream or tan-coloured sedan.

Once in the car, Kemper took the hapless young girl on a bewildering tour of San Francisco's freeways, then pulled a gun on her – this time a .357 Magnum. He told her he was not going to hurt her, but he was suicidal and needed someone to talk to. Then he drove her into the mountains. There he taped her mouth shut and pinched her nostrils until she suffocated. Once she was dead, he raped her inert body and put it in the trunk of the car.

A few miles away, he stopped at a country bar for a few beers. Outside the bar, he opened the trunk to make sure she was dead. 'I suppose as I was standing there looking, I was doing one of those triumphant things, too, admiring my work and admiring her beauty, and I might say admiring my catch like a fisherman,' he said. He felt an exhilaration at the sight of the body. 'I just wanted the exaltation over the party. In other words, winning over death,' he said. 'They were dead and I was alive. That was the victory in my case.'

He drove to see his mother, then took Aiko's body back to his apartment to dismember it. The following day, he drove back to Santa Cruz County where he disposed of the body parts in the mountains – though for the next few days he kept Aiko's head in the trunk of his car.

For Kemper, the decapitation was the best bit. 'I remember it was very exciting,' he said. 'There was actually a sexual thrill ... It was kind of an exalted, triumphant type thing, like taking the head of a deer or an elk or something would be to a hunter. I was the hunter and they were the victims.'

Aiko Koo's head was still in the trunk of his car when he drove to Fresno for a meeting with a couple of court psychiatrists. They were so pleased with his progress that they recommended his juvenile record be sealed. In November, a court confirmed this judgement. Meanwhile, Aiko Koo had been written off by the police as another runaway. Her head was buried along with the body near a religious camp in the Sierra.

Kemper's arm had still not healed and he was running out of money. In December, he moved back to his mother's house in Aptos and returned to the Jury Room to drink with the cops. There, he got the additional thrill of hearing them discuss the missing girls.

On 8 January 1973, Kemper bought a gun, a .22 automatic. There was no problem as he now had a clean record. 'I went bananas after I got that .22,' he said.

That evening he drove up to the Santa Cruz campus on the hill above the town. His mother had given him an employee's sticker so that he could drive on and off the campus without problem. It was raining and there was no shortage of girls looking for lifts down to the town.

He picked up two or three students that night but, concerned that they might have been seen getting into his car, he took them where they wanted to go. He had given up the hunt for that night and was on his way home when he saw 19-year-old Cindy Schall hitching a ride in the town itself. She was a trainee teacher who had been babysitting and was now on her way back to Cabrillo Community College. On the way, Kemper pulled out his gun and told her the same story he had told Aiko.

He drove her out to the small town of Freedom in the hills. There he stopped and ordered her at gunpoint to get into the trunk of the car. As she got in, he shot her in the head. She died instantly.

His mother was out for the evening, so Kemper took her body home and hid it in a cupboard in his bedroom. Cindy's blood had splashed on the plaster cast on his arm. He covered it with shoe whitener and settled down in front of the TV until his mother came home.

In the morning, when his mother had gone to work, he got out Cindy's corpse and sexually assaulted it. Then he took it into the bathroom where he cut it up. He put the head back in the cupboard. The rest of the body was put into plastic sacks; these were loaded into the car. Then he drove down to Monterrey where he threw the sacks over a cliff into the sea.

The next day, one of the bags washed ashore. It was spotted by a Highway Patrolman; an arm was sticking out of it. Enough of her body was recovered for her to be identified.

The off-duty cops in the Jury Room discussed the case, little suspecting that their friend Ed was the culprit. Happy to buy them drinks, Kemper got an informal briefing about the progress of the investigation.

Hearing that some of Cindy Schall's remains had been found, he panicked. Hanging around with policemen, he had learnt about ballistics and the identification of bullets. As he had used his own gun, he dug the bullet out of Cindy's head and buried the head in a flowerbed in the back garden, facing towards the house. He even remarked to his mother, casually, 'People really look up to you around here'. Even more weirdly, he admitted later, 'Sometimes at night, I talked to her, saying love things, the way you do to a girlfriend or wife.'

Less than a month later, on 5 February, Kemper had another violent row with his mother. He stormed out, saying that he was going to a movie. Instead, he drove back to the Santa Cruz campus with murderous intent. 'My mother and I had had a real tiff,' he said. 'I was pissed. I told her I was going to a movie and I jumped up and went straight to the campus because it was still early. I said, "The first girl that's halfway decent that I pick up, I'm gonna blow her brains out.'"

It was another wet night, so there were plenty of possibilities. He picked up Rosalind Thorpe as she came out of a lecture and decided that the 24-year-old linguistics student would make an ideal victim. 'Circumstances were perfect,' he said later. 'Nobody else was around, the guard didn't notice me coming in, nothing would look unusual going out, and she was not the least bit suspecting.'

As he drove off the campus, Kemper spotted another girl hitching a ride. He stopped and Rosalind got out so that 23-year-old Alice Liu could get into the back seat. Rosalind got back in the front seat and he drove off with the two girls.

The road from the university down to the town of Santa Cruz descends in a series of sweeping curves with views over the ocean and the city lights below. Kemper slowed to walking pace, reached down, pulled out his gun and shot Rosalind in the head. She slumped forward against her seatbelt.

Alice was now trapped in the back. She dodged as he tried to shoot her. The first two bullets missed as he was shooting with his right hand. He was left-handed, but his left arm was in a cast. The third bullet hit Alice in the temple. She lay still as he covered her with a blanket and, with Rosalind leaning against his shoulder, he passed through the security check at the edge of the campus. For Kemper, it was the ultimate thrill to get away with his ghastly crimes right under the nose of the law.

He drove out of town and stopped in a quiet road, where he stashed the bodies in the boot. Driving home, he ate dinner and waited for his mother to go to bed. Then he went out to the car and opened the trunk. There, in the street, he cut off their heads with a hunting knife and removed the bullets. He carried Liu's headless body into the house and raped it on the floor. Then he returned it to the car, chopping the hands off the corpses as an afterthought.

Kemper did not bother to cut up the corpses any further – the thrill had gone. But he still had to get rid of them. He decided to drive up to the San Francisco area and dump them there. When they were found, he thought the police would assume that they had been killed by a local man.

He had a friend who lived in northern California and went to visit him. After midnight, he dumped his victims' bodies in Eden Canyon. Then he drove on to the coast and threw the girls' heads and hands over a cliff called Devil's Slide.

The bodies were found a week later. When they were identified, the murders were linked to that of Cindy Schall and Mary Guilfoyle, another student from Cabrillo College whose body had been found that January. She had been the victim of another serial killer named Herbert Mullin, who was doing the rounds in California at the time. By then, Mullin had killed 13.

From his police friends, Kemper knew the hunt was on. He became a bundle of nerves and developed stomach ulcers. It was time, he decided, to carry out one last bloody act. He fantasised about murdering everyone on the block as 'a demonstration to the authorities,' he said later, 'that he was not a man to be trifled with.' He would sneak around at night and kill as many people as possible before he was stopped.

There was one problem with this – mass murderers who go about their business that way end up getting cornered, then are either shot down by the authorities or kill themselves. He did not want to die. Then his thoughts turned to his mother. How could she cope with knowing that he had killed all those girls? It was a weapon he could use against her.

'There were times when she was bitching and yelling at me,' he said, 'that I felt like retaliating and walking over to the telephone in her presence and calling the police, to say, "Hello … I'm the Co-ed Killer," just to lay it on her.'

In the end, he said he killed his mother to spare her the suffering and shame that knowledge of his crimes would bring. In his view, it was an act of mercy.

In the week before Easter, he went back to see his old flatmate in the apartment in Alameda and put in some time at his old job. Finishing work on Good Friday, 20 April, he drove back to Aptos. His mother had gone out after work so, alone, he sat drinking and watching TV. At midnight he went to bed, but slept only fitfully. Each time he woke, he padded along to his mother's room to see if she had come home.

She eventually turned up at 4.00am. They talked briefly, then he went back to bed. He lay there until 5.00am, when he was sure she would be asleep. Then he walked quietly back to her bedroom carrying a hammer and a penknife. For a while, he watched her sleeping. Then he raised the hammer and brought it down on her head with all the force he could muster. She did not stir, but she was still breathing. He turned her over on to her back and slit her throat. Then he cut her head off and raped her headless corpse. The final bloody act was to cut out her larynx and shove it down the garbage disposal unit.

'It seemed appropriate,' he said, 'as much as she'd bitched and screamed and yelled at me over so many years.'

He propped her severed head up on the mantelpiece and screamed at it for an hour. Then he threw darts at it and, finally, smashed her face in.

The deed was done, but Kemper did not feel the usual sense of relief he felt after he had killed. He felt terrible. Only then did it dawn on him that her workmates were going to start asking questions when she did not turn up to work after the Easter holiday.

He decided to tell her friends and colleagues that she had gone away. It would make this more plausible, he thought, if one of her friends had gone with her and both disappeared at the same time. So he phoned Sally Hallett, a woman in her late fifties who worked with his mother at the university and was fairly friendly with her. He told Mrs Hallett that he was arranging a surprise dinner for his mother to celebrate his return to work and invited her over.

When she arrived, he overpowered her. 'I came up behind her and crooked my arm around her neck,' he said. 'I squeezed and just lifted her off the floor. She just hung there and, for a moment, I didn't realise she was dead. I had broken her neck and her head was just wobbling around with the bones of her neck disconnected in the skin sack of her neck.' He then cut off her head and deposited her body in bed. Afterwards, he went to the Jury Room for a drink. Returning, he went to sleep in his mother's bed.

Waking on Easter Sunday, he decided that there was nothing left to do but make a run for it. He had, after all, broken a number of his own rules. He had killed when angry and had kept the weapon and some of his victims' possessions, even some of their body parts. Now he had killed two people who could be directly connected to him.

By then, he had built up a considerable arsenal. He loaded this into the trunk of his Ford Galaxie before heading off eastwards. America was a big country and he was sure he could get lost in it. Keeping himself awake with Coca-Cola and caffeine tablets, he drove on through Sunday night and Monday.

As he drove, he listened to the radio, expecting to hear news of the discovery of the bodies of his mother and Mrs Hallett. There was none and he did not know whether to be please or disappointed. By midnight on 23 April, he was over the Rocky Mountains. As fatigue kicked in, his mood swung wildly from elation to despair. Desperation began to creep in. Even America was not big enough to escape from what he had done.

With nowhere to hide, he figured that he risked being killed if he kept on running. In the small town of Pueblo,

Colorado, he pulled over at a payphone and called the Santa Cruz Police Department to confess. The officers there were his drinking buddies from the Jury Room and did not believe what he was saying. They thought he was making a crank call and the duty officer told him to call back in the morning.

At 5.00am, he rang back. Again, he spoke to someone whom he knew from the Jury Room. Kemper told him that he had killed eight people and was now in Pueblo, Colorado. 'I have over 200 rounds of ammo in the trunk and 3 guns,' he said, 'I don't even want to go near it.'

The officer kept him talking while a colleague called the police in Colorado. The conversation was still in full flow when the officer said that the phone booth was now surrounded by armed men and he should come out with his hands up.

Once in custody, Kemper waived his right to an attorney and began a detailed confession, which was taped. It continued when he was returned to Santa Cruz. He even admitted to slicing the flesh from the legs of at least two of his victims and cooking it in a macaroni casserole. Eating their flesh, Kemper said, was his means of 'possessing' his prey. He also admitted to removing teeth, along with bits of hair and skin as grisly keepsakes. They were the trophies of his hunt.

After he had finished his confession, he went out with detectives – shadowed at a distance by newspaper men – to find the parts of the bodies that had not already been discovered. The police were photographed digging at the back garden of his mother's house in Aptos to retrieve Cindy Schall's head.

He surrendered the other murder weapons he had and handed over the women's personal possessions that he had kept. Forensic teams also found bloodstains in his car, further corroborating his story.

After his arrest, he made four suicide attempts, once slashing his arteries with the metal casing of a ballpoint pen left in a folder of court papers. He tried to kill himself, he said, not because he did not like being locked up, but because the 'kindness and respect with which I was treated by the people after a while started to get to me. I started feeling like I didn't deserve all that nice treatment after what I had done. And I guess that's why I started cutting myself up.'

As Kemper had openly admitted to the crimes, the only course of action open to the public defender, James Jackson, was to enter an insanity plea. Kemper agreed as he was eager to go back to Atascadero.

'After all, I grew up there,' said Kemper. 'That used to be, like, my home. Basically, I was born there, you know. I have a lot of fond memories of the place and I don't know anybody else who has. I felt I definitely could have done a lot of good there, helping people return to the streets ... I could have fitted in there quicker than anybody else.'

Kemper had been diagnosed as a schizophrenic before. But the reputation of psychiatry was at an all-time low in California. Herbert Mullin had just been convicted of two murders in the first degree and eight in the second degree.

He, too, had been diagnosed as a paranoid schizophrenic earlier, committed to a mental hospital and released to kill 13 people. He had also admitted his crimes, but a jury had found him to be sane and culpable because he had shown premeditation.

For Kemper, the trial was just 'a matter to decide by which method I won't see society again. And I certainly wouldn't trust me in society again,' he said.

The jury was played his taped confessions and both sides brought in expert psychiatric witnesses. His sister Allyn related some of the bizarre incidents from her brother's childhood. She said that both she and her mother had suspected that Ed was the Co-ed Killer, especially when they heard that the victims had been decapitated.

Kemper took the stand to talk about his interior life. Giving testimony he appeared shy and awkward, a stark contrast to the wisecracking braggart the jury had heard on the tapes. On the stand, he was sheepish; on the tapes, he revelled in the grisly details of what he had done. He admitted that, in his fantasies, he had made two of the girls 'a part of me' by eating 'parts of them'. All his co-ed victims, he said, 'were like spirit wives. I still had their spirits. I still have them.'

Under cross-examination, he admitted fantasising about killing 'thousands of people', including District Attorney Peter Chang himself. When asked what he thought his punishment should be, he said quietly, 'Death by torture.'

At one point, he had even said that, if he was sent to prison, he would kill someone so that he could die in the gas chamber. 'I wanted to kill "Herbie" Mullin, my fellow mass murderer,' he said later. 'There was a time when I thought it would be a good solution for everyone. It would be good for society and save everyone a bundle of money. Instead of spending thousands and thousands of dollars to lock the two of us up for life to protect us from people and people from us, I figured that if I killed Mullin and then they sent me to the gas chamber, it would be a good solution to the problem. I know I'd never get a chance to, though, and I don't have any intention of killing him or anyone else.'

Kemper and Mullin had been held in adjacent cells in San Mateo County Jail and Kemper made no secret of his contempt for his fellow mass murderer. 'You are a no-class killer,' he said when they first met.

Under questioning from Chang, Kemper admitted he had thrown water through the cell bars on to Mullin to 'shut him up when he was disturbing everybody by singing off-key in his high-pitched, squeaky voice.' Kemper added, 'When he was a good boy, I gave him peanuts. He liked peanuts.'

The alternate water treatment and the peanuts, Kemper said, 'was behavioural modification treatment. The jailers were very pleased with me.'

James Jackson made an eloquent plea on behalf of his client. 'There are two people locked up in the body of this young giant – one good and one evil,' he said. 'One is fighting to be here with us and the other is slipping off to his own little world of fantasy where he is happy.'

It made no difference. The jury took just five hours to find Ed Kemper guilty on all eight counts of murder. The death penalty in California was suspended at the time, so he was sentenced to life imprisonment. The judge recommended that he should never be freed. There was no appeal. In jail, he said, he was happy to be 'locked up in a little room where I can't hurt anybody and I'll be left to my own fantasies.'

Interviewed after his conviction by Marj von Beroldingen of *Front Page Detective* magazine, Kemper still vied with Mullin. 'It really sticks in my craw that Mullin only got two "firsts" and I got eight,' he said. 'He was just a cold-blooded killer, running over a three-week period killing everybody he saw for no good reason ... I guess that's kind of hilarious, my sitting here so self-righteously talking like that after what I've done.'

At the end of the interview, Kemper told von Beroldingen, 'You haven't asked the questions I expected a reporter to ask.' Asked for some examples, Kemper said, 'Oh, what is it like to have sex with a dead body? What does it feel like to sit on your living room couch and look over and see two decapitated girls' heads on the arm of the couch?'

Volunteering the answer, he said, 'The first time, it makes you sick to your stomach.'

Another question he expected to be asked was, 'What do you think, now, when you see a pretty girl walking down the street?' Again, he answered his own question: 'One side of me says, "Wow, what an attractive chick. I'd like to talk to her, date her." The other side of me says, "I wonder how her head would look on a stick?"'

When Kemper left court, he handed his cherished Junior Chamber of Commerce pin to Santa Cruz County Sheriff's Deputy Bruce Colomy, who had transported Kemper back and forth between San Mateo County Jail and Santa Cruz for court appearances and stayed with him at all times when he was out of his cell. 'He's more like a father to me than anyone I have ever known,' said Kemper. 'He's like the father I wish I had had.'

Confined in the state prison at Vacaville, he joined a volunteer group of prisoners recording books for the blind. By 1987, he had made some 5,000 hours of recording, more than any other prisoner. At least six applications for parole have been turned down.

9

THE GIRLFRIEND'S GARDEN

On 25 April 1992, Sharon Thompson returned home to her terraced house in Greening Street, Abbey Wood, to find her boyfriend, 24-year-old delivery driver Benjamin Laing, there. He was tired, sweaty and dishevelled, and told her that he had been digging over her back garden for her. Four days later, Laing was arrested and charged with fraud. Two days after that, he was charged with kidnapping 62-year-old widower Matthew Manwaring and his 23-year-old daughter Alison. It was then that Sharon Thompson called the police.

Within hours, a team of officers arrived. A neighbour confirmed that she had seen Laing digging at the end of the garden with a pickaxe and spade in the pouring rain the previous week. Forensic experts erected a plastic tent over a large patch of recently disturbed soil. Using trowels, they slowly scraped away the earth; 2ft down, they found a black plastic bin-liner. There were ten bags in all. They contained the dismembered remains of Matthew and Alison Manwaring.

The bodies had been beheaded and their limbs had been cut off using a Stanley knife and a hacksaw blade from Matthew Manwaring's own toolbox. A post-mortem examination revealed that Matthew had been shot at point-blank range. The blast from a shotgun had ripped through his head; his daughter had been strangled. Laing was charged with two counts of murder.

The tale of their horrendous end had begun innocently enough when Matthew Manwaring, a retired bank messenger, put a small ad for a Ford Escort Cabriolet XR3i in his local newspaper. It belonged to his son, an RAF fighter pilot, who was away on exercises in Greece. The paper came out on 23 April and had been on the streets for only a few hours when a potential buyer phoned to ask whether the car was still for sale. Told that it was, the caller said that he could drop by in the morning to look at the car. Mr Manwaring gave him his address in Aldersey Gardens, Barking, east London.

At 10.30pm, Matthew was getting ready for bed when there was a knock at the door. The caller was a young man in his mid-twenties. He apologised, saying that he was the man who had called earlier. He had found himself in Barking that evening and asked if it was too late to see the car. A neighbour saw the two men talking on the doorstep before they went into the semi-detached house.

The following morning, the Manwaring's G-registered

Cabriolet was gone. Six miles away in Hornchurch, Matthew Manwaring's brother Derek was waiting for him; they were going trout fishing. He phoned his brother's house; there was no reply.

In Forest Gate, four miles west of Barking, the staff at the bank where Alison Manwaring worked were wondering why she had not come in. She had not phoned in sick and she was usually so reliable.

Alison lived with her widowed father, but she was supposed to be moving into a new home with her fiancé, hospital worker Gordon Healis, in a few days' time. He was surprised to hear that she was not there when he called her work. They had spent the previous evening together, measuring the windows of their new home for curtains. She had left at around 10.30pm to drive back to her father's house in her Mini Metro.

Gordon, too, called the house and got no reply. Again, no one answered when he called that evening. He grew concerned.

Derek had a key to his brother's house so, on Saturday 25 April, Gordon and Derek let themselves in. The curtains were drawn and the lights were off; no one answered their calls. A quick look round convinced them that there was no one home and they left, baffled.

On Sunday, Derek went back to the house. It was still deserted. Now deeply worried, Gordon and Derek returned again on Monday, 27 April. This time they turned on the lights and opened the curtains. To their horror, they found Matthew Manwaring's armchair and the carpet in front of it soaked with blood. Immediately they called the police.

DS Mike Morgan from Scotland Yard's Major Incident Pool and DI Phil Burrows from Barking CID arrived. They swiftly concluded that something very nasty indeed had taken place in Aldersey Gardens. Apart from the blood on the armchair and carpet, they found blood-soaked cushion covers in the washing machine. Someone had made a half-hearted attempt to wash them.

In the bathroom, they found that the bath had been cleaned, but there were still spots of blood around it. The frame of the door leading from the hall into the living room had been broken. Someone had tried to repair it crudely with filler and paint, but they could still see shotgun pellets embedded in the timber. Clearly, there had been a shooting.

They also found a note in Alison Manwaring's handwriting. It was addressed to Gordon Healis, saying that she and her father had gone away for a few days. She would explain why later. But why would Alison have left a note for Gordon inside the house when she must have known that he did not have a key? It was clear from the wording that she had been forced to write it.

Alongside the note was a handwritten receipt for £7,750 in cash for the sale of the red Cabriolet. The buyer, it said, was a Mr Sinclair. Both the Escort and Alison's Metro were missing, along with jewellery, a camera, cheque books, a building society account book and other items.

The police decided to hold a press conference. On the morning of 29 April, the story of the missing father and daughter made headlines in the national newspapers. DS Morgan would only say that they had disappeared in 'strange and suspicious circumstances'. However, they would like to interview a young man, possibly of mixed race, with a moustache and goatee, who had been seen talking to Matthew Manwaring beside his son's car.

That afternoon, a tall, powerfully built mixed-race man with a goatee and wispy moustache walked into Barking Police Station. It was Benjamin Laing, a delivery driver for Selfridges. He said that he had read in the newspapers that he had been seen talking to Matthew Manwaring and said that he had gone to the house after seeing the advertise-ment offering a car for sale in the local paper. He had bought the Cabriolet for £7,750 and had taken it away that night. When he had left Aldersey Gardens, Mr Manwaring and his daughter were alive and well, he said. That was all he knew.

DI Burrows asked where the car was. Laing said that he had already sold it at an auction in Enfield, north London, on Monday. But Burrows had an ace up his sleeve. When they discovered the cheque books and building society books were missing, they alerted every bank and building society in London and Essex. On Friday 24 April, a man answering Laing's description had walked into a branch of the Nationwide Building Society and tried to withdraw £200. But the signature on the withdrawal slip did not match the one in the book. Suspecting a fraud, the cashier switched on the hidden surveillance camera before refusing to hand over the cash. Laing had been videoed.

When he was told this, Laing was shaken, but quickly regained his composure. He said that he had found the building society book in the car manual inside the Escort.

'It was among the documents for the car,' he said. 'I don't know how it got there. OK, I tried to get some money with it, but that's all.'

When the CID checked the records at Scotland Yard, they found that Laing had five previous convictions for armed robbery; they had taken place in 1987 when he was still a teenager and were all fairly petty – he had used a replica pistol to rob taxi drivers.

With this, Benjamin Laing had thrown away a promising life. Born in Paisley, he was the son of Kojo Laing, a leading author and poet in his native Ghana. Benjamin had an IQ of 150. With ten O-levels and four A-levels, he had been offered a place at Loughborough University. Instead, he was sentenced to six years' youth custody and released in 1990 after serving less than half his sentence. Unable to resume his academic career, he took a job as a £150-a-week van driver.

Although DI Burrows was convinced that the Manwarings were dead and that he was looking at the killer, Laing was only charged with attempted fraud and remanded in custody in Pentonville Prison.

Detectives contacted the auction site in Enfield. They confirmed that they had sold the Escort; Laing had used his own name. That was why he had been forced to come forward; he had taken £7,600 for it. After the auctioneer's commission, Laing had only got £7,000 – a loss of £750.

The police tracked down the dealer who had bought the car. When they examined it, they found that the carpet in the boot was still damp with blood. It matched the blood found in the house. It seemed that Laing had killed his victims and used their own car to dispose of the bodies.

Laing lived in East Ham Manor Way, Becton, just two miles from the Manwarings. He had given one of his neighbours a camera to look after. It matched the one missing from the Manwaring's house.

When Laing's home was searched, they found exercise books spelling out his diabolical plot. It was difficult getting money by stealing cars, he wrote, because it was hard to sell them afterwards without the appropriate ownership documents. To get round this, he planned to study the small ads in the local papers and look for suitable victims, preferably someone old and frail. Matthew Manwaring fitted the bill.

Laing's plan was to pretend to be a genuine buyer. Once the ownership documents had been produced, he would kill the victim and make it look like suicide. His idea was to stage a suicide by sealing the victim in a van filled with carbon monoxide. He wrote: 'Let owner call a "friend" from van on mobile phone – have not decided if just owner or family will be in van.' He then wrote a shopping list of things he would need. His murder kit included bin-liners, handcuffs, a crossbow and a pump-action shotgun.

The case was building against Laing. But still there was no direct evidence proving that Laing had killed Matthew and Alison Manwaring.

Before the bodies were found, Mark Manwaring had flown home from Greece to launch an appeal for information on the whereabouts of his sister and father. Soon after he arrived home, a letter came for him at his father's home in Aldersey Gardens. It purported to have come from Alison and read:

Dearest Mark,

I know you are very worried about where we are. I cant begin to explain the thought that had gone into daddy and I leaving. It has been very very lonely for daddy since mum died and all he does now is drink himself to sleep every night – I cant live with him in that state so we both decided to have a break and try to forget the constant pain.

The – sorry for the mistakes, im still a bit nervous – last straw was on Thursday night after we sold the car and daddy was so drunk he fell down and cut his chest. He is alright now though and trying to forget the loneliness. I promise you Mark im looking after him well.

Mark, we took some photos, my sentimental jewelry, the car money, our bank books – I think we took yours by mistake too. Please understand the way we had to do things – Its but necessary, for daddy.

I can't tell you where we are yet, but we are in London still. I swear to you we are ok. I left my car behind plaistow station, you would have traced us too quickly so Daddy said to leave it.

Daddy needs to be happy again Mark and ill do it for him. Please understand – we both love you so much and its hard to ask you to understand but try to for now. Once Daddy sorts out his feelings and I feel better about the termination I had to have – It hurts too much to go into that now... We will send photographs from Daddy's camera when we develop them.

Love Always in God.

DADDY and ALISON

Even the signatures were typed.

Alison had never told anyone in her family that she had had an abortion. The police believe that Laing had forced it out of her when she came home. And no one besides the murderer knew he had been injured in the chest. But it was with this letter that Laing convicted himself. Plainly, it had been concocted by him and given to a sympathetic friend to deliver. In it, he had arrogantly given his name away. The sign-off line – 'Love Always in God' – spelt out Laing.

Alison's car was found behind Plaistow Station. Laing was now charged with kidnapping and made a brief court appearance. It was then that the police heard from his girlfriend, Sharon Thompson.

When the bodies were unearthed, Laing blamed the Fijian Freedom Fighters, a terrorist organisation that did not exist, for their murder. Meanwhile, a police team were making a fingertip search of Cyprus Place, scrubland in London's then derelict Docklands near Laing's home. After a few days, they found two sets of handcuffs and were able to trace them back to the shop where Laing had bought them shortly before the murders. They also found bin-liners containing Alison's jewellery and other property stolen from the Manwarings' home, along with Matthew

Manwaring's driving licence that had been torn into eight pieces. But they had yet to find the gun.

After a lengthy interrogation of Sharon Thompson, she admitted that Laing had hidden it under the stairs in her house. While the police were searching for it in Cyprus Place, she had told Laing's best friend, 21-year-old Mark Leslie, where it was hidden. He moved it to a safer hiding place. Then Laing's brother Peter took the gun and threw it in the Thames.

He eventually led the police to where he had disposed of it and police divers retrieved the firearm. The murder weapon was a single-barrelled automatic that had been sawn off. At a hearing in May 1993, Sharon Thompson, Mark Leslie and Peter Laing all pleaded guilty to handling the gun and were given a conditional discharge. A charge of conspiring to pervert the course of justice was left on file.

The police then pieced together the clues to discover what had befallen Matthew Manwaring and his daughter. They believed that Laing arrived with his 'implements of murder and torture' in a guitar case. After letting Laing into his home, Matthew Manwaring was pushed back into his armchair, then shot in the chest at close range. The muzzle flash burnt the skin and the surrounding flesh was peppered with shotgun pellets.

Alison arrived home about an hour later, while Laing was trying to clear up the blood. Laing fired into the doorframe to frighten her. Then he got her to write a bogus receipt for £7,750 for the Escort and sign several cheques. She was forced to tell him the PIN for her cash card and tell him details of her private life. She was then made to write the bogus note to her fiancé Gordon Healis.

Laing made her strip naked, gagged her, tied her ankles together and handcuffed her to a radiator. He then sexually assaulted her.

'Laing subjected her to all manner of degradation,' said DS Morgan. 'He repeatedly beat Alison around the head and face. He tortured and raped her to satisfy his needs for power and control. He enjoyed having someone's life in his hands.'

Her suffering continued until he finally strangled her with his bare hands. Then he put her body in the bath, cut her head off and dismembered the body with a selection of butcher's knives. He repeated the grisly procedure with her father. The body parts were put in bin-liners and carried out to the boot of the Escort. After he washed away most of the blood and made crude repairs to the doorframe, he drove to some wasteland, where he dumped them.

The next day, he used the car to drive friends out to Alton Towers in Staffordshire for a day out. Detectives found pictures of him laughing as he rode the giant water chute. At the weekend, he hired a Vauxhall Astra and drove back to the waste ground and recovered the bodies. Then he drove them to Sharon Thompson's house and buried them in her back garden. He had tried to hire a mechanical digger for the task, but to save money he borrowed a shovel from Mark Leslie.

Laing was twice tested for insanity before the trial opened at the Old Bailey on 24 February 1993. He pleaded not guilty to both murder charges. Prosecuting, Michael Stuart-Moore QC told the jury that Matthew and Alison Manwaring had been murdered simply for the paltry sum he could raise from selling their car and rifling their bank and building society accounts. 'Perhaps the motive is so obscene as to be unspeakable,' he said. 'It may be you cannot believe that anyone would do, for the sake of a motor car and a few bank books, what I have described just out of sheer greed. What Laing did in order to get his way involved the destruction of a family.'

While Matthew Manwaring had been despatched cleanly, Alison was made to suffer. 'Alison's fate that night and the ordeal she went through can be pieced together from a large number of terrible clues,' said the prosecutor. 'She was strangled to death, but not before she went through some form of mental torture or duress. She was physically assaulted as well. Her hands were manacled to render her even more helpless than she already was.'

Stuart-Moore said that the bogus letter Laing had sent Mark Manwaring was one of the more extraordinary features of the case. It had been designed to put the police and family off the scent, but he had revealed himself in the line 'Love Always in God'. 'It illustrated the total arrogance of the man who killed Mark's sister and father and believed he could get away with that crime,' he said. 'Had he been acquitted, he would have had the last laugh. He never intended it to be noticed and it nearly did go unnoticed.'

When he took the stand, Laing maintained that the blueprint for murder found in his home were notes for a book his father wanted to write about revenge. The central characters were a car salesman and a customer.

'I suggested that the customer set up the salesman in a suicide set-up, then sold his car and bought his business,' he said.

The shopping list was 'a disposal list, to remind me of things I had to get rid of. Things that could connect me to the murder,' he said.

He told the court he had been framed for the murder by Mark Leslie, his best friend, Neil Philips, another friend, and Frank Cohen, a car thief. He said Leslie had confessed to him that Cohen had murdered the Manwarings, while he watched. 'Mark told me what happened ... the murderer is a monster.'

Although Mr Laing admitted to buying two pairs of handcuffs the day before the murders, he said they were for Mark Leslie. He denied manacling Alison Manwaring to a bedroom radiator and torturing her to reveal banking information and personal details. Four days after the murder, Laing said, Leslie and Cohen buried the dismembered bodies in his girlfriend's garden. He denied a neighbour's allegation that she had seen him digging the graves. 'She couldn't have meant me, she knows me. I am not white, the only white person is Frank,' he said.

Stuart-Moore suggested that Cohen was a figment of Laing's vivid imagination. He added, 'For Frank Cohen, we should read Benjamin Ekow Laing.'

It took the jury of six men and six women four hours to find Laing guilty as charged. There were cheers from the public gallery. Mark Manwaring punched the air, while Gordon Healis wept uncontrollably.

The judge, Justice Robert Lymbery, sentenced Laing to life, recommending that the serve at least 25 years. 'Whether the Home Secretary will then find it safe to release you must be a matter for him,' the judge said. 'He should be on his guard. You are a dangerous man, capable of extreme violence. You are capable of deceit and dishonesty. You are utterly ruthless and have a clever and able mind.'

DS Michael Morgan said, 'The ease with which he dismembered the bodies of these two innocent victims was particularly horrific. He is an arrogant and calculating killer and I am convinced he would have struck again.'

10

PUSHER UNDER
THE PATIO

In February 1999, the police investigating the murder of
drug dealer Arthur 'Joe the Crow' Rouse found his body
encased in concrete under a patio in west London. They
also dug up the garden, believing that up to six people were
buried there, including hitman Gilbert Wynter who vanished
in 1998.

An officer said, 'There may be other bodies buried in the
same area. Several gangland characters have gone missing
in the past year or two. We think they may have gone to
the same resting place as Joe the Crow.'

Forty-four-year-old Rouse had been blasted at close
range in the face and stomach with a shotgun. Police
believed he was killed after leaving his home in Chiswick,
west London, in September 1998, to meet a man to settle
a dispute over a £50,000 drug deal. He was never seen
alive again. Relatives reported him missing in January

when he failed to show up to a family party on New Year's Eve.

Police found his remains in the garden in Perivale after digging up the patio, which appeared to have been recently laid. They went there the day after armed officers, acting on a tip-off, ambushed a man near a house in Old Windsor, in the shadow of Windsor Castle. When they searched him, officers found he was carrying a loaded sawn-off shotgun in a custom-made shoulder holster.

The house belonged to Thomas 'Tommy the Gun' Green who had dug the makeshift grave with his nephew Jack Lang and laid concrete over it. They then went to stay at a hotel in Newquay where they celebrated with vintage champagne. They were arrested there by armed police. Green was jailed for life for the murder of Rouse. Lang pleaded guilty to perverting the course of justice by hiding the corpse and to two offences of selling cocaine.

11

BLOCK HEAD

The head of 54-year-old Susan Craven was destined for the patio, said Kenneth Peatfield, her lover, who was convicted of her murder. But it did not make it there. Police found it encased in a 2-ft concrete block before the new patio was completed.

Mrs Craven had met Peatfield after he had shared a cell with her millionaire car-breaker husband, Alan, who was inside for dealing in stolen parts. Fifty-year-old Peatfield, a heating engineer with Bury Council, was then serving ten years for trying to hire a hitman to murder his ten-year-old daughter Helen and wife Janet, whose life was insured for £50,000.

The double-murder plot began when Peatfield casually asked a man in a pub if he could 'fix' the killings of Janet and Helen. He said that he 'was not bothered' how it was done. Over pints of beer in his local pub, Peatfield told hitman Bernard 'Mr Bright' Chadderton to make the murders look like a bungled burglary. He offered Chadderton a £5,000 deposit, with another £45,000 when the job was done. But the hitman was appalled by his callousness and went to the police saying he was 'sickened and frightened'. The next time they met, at the Flying Horse pub in Rochdale, the conversation was recorded using a hidden microphone.

When Janet discovered what her husband was planning, she was shocked. 'When I learned what happened, I couldn't believe it as Ken was a good father and husband,' she said. 'But he's always been obsessed with money.'

Helen was deeply affected by what happened. She did not speak for months after realising what her father planned to do.

Sentencing him to ten years in jail at Manchester Crown Court, Mr Justice Glidewell said, 'The story I've heard is not merely horrifying, but incredible.'

After he left jail, Peatfield moved in with Susan Craven, who had just reached a £181,000 divorce settlement. They drew up wills leaving everything to each other.

A week later, Peatfield invited Faith Warner, his 17-year-old girlfriend, to the house he shared with Susan. 'I remember that day like it was yesterday,' she said. 'We had been out to buy a gravestone for our child and I was upset. I was nagging him all day and when we got back to his house I said I felt uncomfortable and what if Susan came back while I was there. That's when he told me she'd never be coming back and he took me out to the garden shed.'

In the back garden, he told her, 'I'm going to show you something that will change your life.' Then he pulled back a blue tarpaulin to reveal part of Susan's body and said, 'I did it so I could be with you.'

He wanted to convince his teenage lover that Susan was no longer any obstacle to them being together. But Faith was horrified. 'He grabbed both of my arms, went blood-red, literally, and shook me and said, "If you tell anybody, I will kill you and I will kill your family." I have felt physically sick knowing what he was capable of.'

Peatfield told friends and neighbours that Susan had walked out on him for no apparent reason. But suspicious neighbours knew she would never have left behind her treasured dog, and so they called the police. Spots of blood were found in the house and Peatfield was charged with murder. The following day, detectives decided to crack open the 330-lb block of concrete in the garage.

'Nobody could believe it when the head was found,' said one officer. 'Even the most hardened detectives were utterly appalled.'

The rest of the body was never found.

During the three-week trial, Peatfield tried to accuse Susan's former husband, who is nearly blind, of kidnapping and murdering her, then putting her head in concrete and leaving the block in his garage. The jury didn't believe a word of it.

Sentencing Peatfield to life with a tariff of 18 years at Sheffield Crown Court, Mr Justice Bell told him, 'You murdered the woman with whom you had lived for some years – a woman who needed your support. You murdered her when you were infatuated with a much younger woman who you hoped would come to live with you in Susan Craven's place.'

Susan's son Paul pleaded with Peatfield, 'Come clean and tell us where Mum's body is so that she can be laid to rest.' He added, 'Even 25 years in prison is too good for him. He even tried to drag our family down by shifting the blame. It was all a smokescreen for what he did.'

Peatfield was beaten up in prison and his appeal to have his sentence reduced was thrown out.

With Peatfield safely in jail, Faith spoke out. 'Deep down I know that I was destined to be his next victim,' she said. 'I am haunted by nightmares where I see my own head inside a lump of concrete.'

When their affair began, Faith was completely taken in by her seemingly docile lover. 'At the start of our relationship, he seemed so gentle,' she said. 'Then I saw a side I didn't like. Once, when he was cross, he put his hand on my windpipe and tried to strangle me. Now I know what he can do, I feel physically sick.'

The scales had fallen from her eyes that afternoon in the back garden. 'When Kenneth showed me the body that day I knew that if I stayed with him I would be his next victim,' she said. 'He said that if I told anyone about the body he would kill me and my family. But I knew, no matter what, that one day he would kill me if another girl came into his life. That's when I decided to finish the relationship. I didn't go to the police because I was petrified that he would kill me, my two sisters and mum and dad.'

He had already attacked her once when an argument turned violent. She, thankfully, got a second chance.

12

FAMILY FEUD

Thirty-three-year-old Lee Ford was sentenced to five life terms after pleading guilty to murdering his wife Lesley and four stepchildren and hiding their bodies in a woodshed in his back garden. Two of the bodies were moved after the police called and were re-buried in a field about four miles away.

'For the life of me, I do not even understand why I did what I did,' said Ford. 'If I had planned to do what I did there is no way I would have left them on the property with my kids there.'

His two natural children remained with him in his isolated home at Carnkie, near Helston, Cornwall, throughout the massacre.

Ford's relationship with his wife became violent after she discovered that he was having sex with her 17-year-old daughter Sarah. Ford was also 'openly and forcefully jealous of Sarah as she sought friendship with young men of her own age,' it was said in court.

Lesley Ford became so concerned that she contacted social services. She also sought an injunction and occupation order on the family home. Nigel Pasco QC, prosecuting, said, 'It is very likely that Lesley Ford was very frightened of her husband at times in the months before her murder.'

Jamie Tabor QC, defending, told the court that Ford felt completely isolated in the run-up to the attack, spending a lot of time locked in his garage watching TV. He said he was terrified his wife would leave him, taking the four stepchildren and his two natural children.

Ford told the police he felt Lesley had too much control over his life and they rowed because she objected to him drinking after work. He was also unhappy about being unable to record TV shows because the children were watching other channels.

Lee Ford apparently 'flipped' after a row in the bedroom with his 36-year-old wife about access to the children and smashed her in the face with a rounders bat belonging to his youngest daughter. After that, he went to the garage to cool down. There he found a 2-ft length of rope.

'The next thing I remember is she is lying on the floor dead,' said Ford. 'I do not know why or what went through me.'

Next came the murders of Sarah, 16-year-old Anne-Marie,

14-year-old Steven and 13-year-old Craig. These killings were not done on a whim, or in a frenzy of anger, it appears – they were chillingly calculated.

'The cause of death was given as ligature strangling,' said Pascoe. 'They were garrotted so precisely as to leave little or no bruising and no damage to the structure of the neck. He admitted using a rope from behind to kill each of his victims.'

The four stepchildren were killed in the kitchen. Anne-Marie and Sarah had been dressed casually while the two brothers and Ford's wife had been wearing nightclothes. This was because the murders took place over a 24-hour period.

'Garrotting can be described as a clean and very efficient form of killing,' Pascoe added. 'The Crown asserts that such a killing does give an insight into the degree of detachment and planning the defendant must have used to carry out each murder. On the defendant's account, these murders were not one after the other but over a night and subsequent morning.'

Ford told the police, 'There was no struggle. It was with a rope from behind and they did not know it was coming and none knew another one had gone before. What my own hands had done – what a piece of rope has done – to five people is unbelievable.'

The other two children were spared, seemingly, because they were of his blood.

The date of the murders was fixed by a final text message sent from Sarah's phone on 30 August 2000. Eight days later, a friend from McDonald's, where she worked, texted poignantly, 'Are you still alive?'

On 1 September, the day after the murders, Ford called the Jobcentre to cancel an appointment, saying his family were suffering from food poisoning. After hiding the bodies in the woodshed in the back garden of the bungalow, Ford told friends that his wife had left him after a big row. He borrowed a pickaxe from a friend claiming he had to remove wood from the shed where three of the bodies were later recovered.

Ford tried to return a dog his wife had bought days earlier and told the school that the younger children attended that they would not be returning for the new academic year, saying his wife would not cause a problem. He also tried to revive a relationship with an old flame, claiming 'his wife would not be coming back'.

During September, Ford returned Craig's and Steven's school books and, on 28 September, he made an attempt to cash Sarah's last pay cheque from McDonald's.

After the police first called on 30 September, Ford donned a face mask, wrapped the rotting bodies of Sarah and Anne-Marie with polythene, put them into the boot of his car and drove them out to the fields, where he buried them.

Two days later, he packed the two surviving children off to their grandparents in Telford, Shropshire, intending to return and re-bury the other three bodies. But while he was away, his brother-in-law raised the alarm. When he got back to Helston, he was arrested and taken to

Camborne Police Station for questioning, and had no
further opportunity to move the bodies of his wife and the
two boys. They remained in the woodshed where they
were found.

13

MULTI-FACETED MONSTER

Belgian child molester Marc Dutroux was finally incarcerated after two young girls he had repeatedly raped were released from his cellar in Marcinelle, Belgium, in 1996. It was only then that the bodies of two eight-year-old girls were found buried in the garden of another house belonging to Dutroux. They had starved to death in the cellar where he had sexually abused them.

The two eight-year-olds were Julie Lejeune and Melissa Russo. They had been kidnapped together from Grâce-Hollogne in Belgium on 24 June 1995. Now only did Dutroux sexually abuse the two defenceless children, he produced pornographic videos of their ordeal as well.

While Dutroux admitted raping the two girls, he refused to admit responsibility for their deaths; they had died while he was in jail for four months for stealing a car. He claimed that, before he went to prison on 6 December 1995, he had left instructions with his accomplice, Bernard Weinstein, to feed them. He also said that Weinstein had kidnapped the two girls, admittedly on Dutroux's instructions. Dutroux also said that he was so annoyed at Weinstein's failure to feed the two girls, he had given him barbiturates and buried him alive alongside Julie and Melissa in the garden at Sars-la-Buissière. In due course, his body was found.

Another of Dutroux's accomplices, Michel Lelièvre, admitted kidnapping 17-year-old An Marchal and 19-year-old Eefje Lambreks on 22 August 1995 when the two girls were on a camping trip to the Belgian port of Ostend. Their bodies were found under a garden shed next to another house owned by Dutroux, which had then been occupied by Bernard Weinstein.

At one time, there had been four girls at the house in Marcinelle – Julie and Melissa in the dungeon, with An and Eefje chained up upstairs. Eefje had made several escape attempts. In one, she managed to get out on to the roof, but Dutroux had caught her. Eventually, he found the two older girls so troublesome he drugged them and buried them alive.

Four girls and Weinstein were already dead when 12-year-old Sabine Dardenne was kidnapped on her way to school in Tournai on 28 May 1996. She was cycling past the high wall of the local football stadium when a rusty camper van pulled up beside her. The side door slid open. A man leaned out, plucked her from her bike and threw her in the back. It was all over in a split second.

Sabine tried to fight her abductor off, but was small for

her age and he was a fully grown man. He shoved some pills in her mouth and trussed her up in a blanket. He told her to shut up and nothing would happen to her. After a while, the van stopped and her captors put her in a trunk. It was so small they had to bend her double.

After a couple of minutes, the trunk was opened again and she found herself in a room with 'the man with the moustache'. He took her upstairs, told her to undress and get into one of the bunk beds. Once she was naked, he put a chain around her neck. It was just long enough to allow her to walk to a chamber pot. He left her there overnight.

The following day, he returned and said that her parents had been asked for a ransom of 3 million francs (£60,000) for her return. If they could not raise the money, the kidnappers intended to kill her. In the meantime, he took Polaroid pictures of her naked in her chains. He then took her into another bedroom where there was a double bed and sexually abused her. She could not stop crying, which annoyed him. He seemed to think that she should have enjoyed it. She said later that he did not beat her or rape her then, but the things he did to her were so disgusting that she did not want to think about it.

She complained about being kept naked all the time. Eventually, he gave her back her underwear; then, some time later, he returned her jeans, which she could wear when she went downstairs to eat. But she was regularly taken upstairs for more photo sessions and sexual abuse.

Then she was told that her parents had refused to pay the ransom. As a result, the boss of the supposed kidnap gang had ordered that she be killed. But her captor pretended to be her saviour and said he would hide her in the tiny, airless cellar which was 3-ft wide and 9-ft long. She was put down there in a cage with a stinking mattress. Occasionally, her jailor would go away for days on end, leaving her down there. Otherwise, there would be more nude photographs and 'other things'. Eventually, he raped her and forced her to sleep with him in chains.

The rape had left her haemorrhaging badly and in terrible pain. She was afraid that she was going to die from loss of blood alone in her underground prison, and began to wish that he would finish her off with a bullet in the head.

Her captor, Marc Dutroux, was already a convicted paedophile. Born in Ixelles, Belgium, in 1956, Dutroux was the oldest of five children. His parents, both teachers, emigrated to the Belgian Congo, but returned to Belgium when Dutroux was four. When they separated in 1971, Dutroux stayed with his mother. He married at the age of nineteen and fathered two children; the marriage ended in divorce in 1983. By then, he was having an affair with Michelle Martin. In 1986, Dutroux and Martin were arrested for the abduction and rape of five young girls. Dutroux was sentenced to 13 years; Martin got five. They married while in prison in 1989 and would eventually have three children together after they were both released, after just three years, for good behaviour.

Dutroux was an electrician by trade, but in the mid-1990s he was unemployed and living on welfare in the city of Charleroi, known at the time for its high unemployment. He supplemented his income with muggings, drug dealing and stealing cars that were smuggled into Eastern Europe and sold in Slovakia, Poland and Hungary. But his most lucrative sideline was in the sex trade; he produced and dealt in pornography, and sold young girls into prostitution across Europe. By 1996, he owned seven houses in Belgium. Most of them stood vacant and were the perfect hiding places for the girls he had kidnapped, who were then used in pornographic videos or sold on as prostitutes.

The police knew of his activities. In 1993, an informant reported that Dutroux had offered him over 100,000 Belgian francs (£2,000) to kidnap young girls. In 1995, the same man told the police that Dutroux was building a dungeon in which to keep girls whom he would later sell into prostitution. That year, Dutroux's own mother wrote to prosecutors telling them that her son had been keeping young girls in one of his empty houses. But no one did anything about it.

As her captivity dragged on, Sabine became consumed with despair. There was no one to talk to. It was summertime and she wanted to go out in the sunshine. Dutroux shoved two chairs together and told her she should 'sunbathe' – naked, of course – right there in the front room.

She kept saying that she wanted to see her friends. This had unintended and tragic consequences. One day, he announced that he had brought her a friend. Sabine could hardly believe her ears.

First, she had to endure another 'sunbathing' session. Then she was taken upstairs where she found another girl naked and chained to the bunk, as she had been when she first arrived. The new girl asked Sabine how long she had been there; Sabine said it was 77 days.

The new girl was 14-year-old Laetitia Delhez. Dutroux tried to get her to walk around naked, but she kept putting her clothes back on and he gave up. Soon she joined Sabine down in the cellar. She brought important news; she had seen Sabine's picture on posters that had been pasted up all over the country. Sabine had not been forgotten as she had feared.

Laetitia had been snatched in the town of Bertrix on the French border. She had been walking home from the swimming pool when an old van pulled up alongside her. Dutroux had grabbed her and bundled her though the side door in the same way Sabine had been taken. From Laetitia's description, it seemed that the driver was the same man Sabine had seen.

Laetitia was two years older than Sabine. She had already had her first period, so Dutroux forced her to take contraceptive pills. After the first time Laetitia had been raped and abused, Dutroux suddenly stopped coming to get her. A couple of days passed and they figured that he must have gone away again.

In fact, on 13 August 1996, Dutroux, his wife and the driver Michel Lelièvre had been arrested. There had been a witness to the abduction of Laetitia Delhez who noted down part of the licence-plate number of the van. It matched one registered to Dutroux. A search was made of the house by an officer of the child protection squad, but he found nothing. The door to the cellar had been skilfully concealed.

Two days later, Laetitia and Sabine heard bricks being chipped from the walls. The two girls were terrified. Then they heard Dutroux's voice saying, 'It's me.' But there were other men with him. Fearing the worst, Sabine said that she was not coming out. Laetitia then recognised one of the men who had come into the cellar – he was a policeman from Bertrix. Sabine was still hesitant; she turned to Dutroux and asked if she could leave. He said she could. As they left, both Sabine and Laetitia gave Dutroux a kiss goodbye on the cheek.

Sabine then flung herself on to the nearest policemen and did not want to let him go. Laetitia did the same with the policeman from Bertrix. Then, after 80 days in the dank cellar, Sabine was taken out into the sunshine and fresh air. It was only at the police station that Sabine discovered that the investigators had give up any hope of finding her alive long ago. It was Laetitia the police had been looking for when they visited Dutroux's house.

When Dutroux's various houses were searched, the police found over 300 pornographic videos featuring children; 6,000 hair samples taken from the dungeon were analysed to see if Dutroux had kept other victims there. It was only after that that the four bodies were found in the back garden.

During the investigation, businessman Jean-Michel

Nihoul was arrested. He had organised an orgy at a Belgian château attended by police officers, several government officials, and a former European commissioner. Seven other people were arrested in connection with the paedophile ring, and nine police officers in Charleroi were detained for questioning over possible negligence in the investigation.

There was a massive outcry about the whole affair in Belgium. Demands were made to tighten parole conditions for convicted paedophiles; there was also a call for the reinstatement of the death penalty which had been ended in Belgium just months before Sabine and Laetitia were found.

The outrage boiled over when Jean-Marc Connerotte, the investigating judge in the case, was dismissed for having attended a fund-raising dinner to help the search for missing children. The Belgian Supreme Court decided that this might taint his objectivity in the Dutroux case. As a result, 300,000 people took to the streets of Brussels, dressed in white as a symbol of innocence. This was the largest demonstration in Belgium since the Second World War. There was talk that the government was involved a cover-up and strikes broke out across the country in protest. The prime minister promised to speed up reforms to the judicial system and even the king of Belgium had to speak out on the Dutroux case.

A parliamentary committee investigating the matter published a report saying that failures in the investigation of the paedophile ring meant that the four girls who were dead could have been saved. A complete reorganisation of the Belgian police force was called for.

Meanwhile, the police had made another error. Dutroux was allowed to travel to Neufchâteau to consult files he would use in his forthcoming trial. While there, he knocked out one of his police guards, and struck another so that he fell to the ground and took his gun; then he stole a car and made a break for it with half of the local gendarmerie on his tail. Sabine heard helicopters circling above her school. Another pupil asked her if she was frightened when they heard that Dutroux had escaped. But Sabine was sanguine; she figured that Dutroux would have to be exceptionally stupid to come within a million miles of her. As it was, police officers were sent to patrol the school corridors. Bodyguards were sent to her home but, by the time she returned there after school, Dutroux had already been captured. Taking refuge in a wood, he had given himself up to a forest warden. However, his escape forced the resignation of the state police chief, the minister of justice and the minister of the interior.

After his escape attempt, Dutroux went on trial for assault and theft, and was sentenced to five years. But his trial in connection with Sabine and the other girls was delayed when a magazine in Luxembourg printed the names of 50 alleged paedophiles said to have come from the files of the Dutroux investigation.

Dutroux managed to stall things further by claiming that the Belgian state was violating his human rights. He went to court to demand that he be released from solitary confinement, undergo fewer body searches and be allowed to sleep uninterrupted. This outraged the Belgian people again, considering what he had put his victims through. The state argued that Dutroux was being given special treatment for his own protection.

Then an unauthorised interview was released by a Belgian TV channel. In it, Dutroux was heard to admit incarcerating Julie, Melissa, An and Eefje, effectively admitting his guilt. The authenticity and admissibility of this evidence then had to be examined. These issues meant that his trial for the substantive charges of murder and kidnap was postponed repeatedly. Indeed, it was over seven years before the case came to court.

The trial eventually began on 1 March 2004. There were four defendants – Dutroux, his now ex-wife Martin, Lelièvre and Nihoul. By this time, Dutroux was maintaining that he was merely a pawn in the paedophile ring masterminded by Nihoul. Dutroux claimed the girls he kidnapped were to be sold on to Nihoul who then supplied the paedophiles. To muddy the water further, Dutroux claimed that two police officers helped in the kidnapping of An Marchal and Eefje Lambrecks.

The investigating judge Jacques Langlois then alleged that it was Michelle Martin who had left Julie and Melissa to starve, not Weinstein. She had been afraid to go down into the cellar to feed them in case they attacked her, although she claimed she had no idea how or why they had died.

Jean-Marc Connerotte then testified that Dutroux had constructed the dungeon and its ventilation system so well that it would have been difficult to detect the girls' presence even with sniffer dogs. He also testified that his investigation had been hampered by people in government, and that contracts had been taken out against investigating magistrates. He needed armed guards and bulletproof vehicles to protect him from powerful individuals who did not want the truth to come out. And he blamed incompetence of the police in Charleroi for the deaths of Julie Lejeune and Melissa Russo.

The failure of the Belgian authorities was demonstrated again when a key to Dutroux's handcuffs was found in his cell, having been smuggled in, apparently, in a bag of salt. Some of the staff involved in the prison were then accused to trying to organise his escape.

The final showdown came on 19 April 2004, when Sabine Dardenne, now aged 20, took the stand. She told of the ordeal to which she had been subjected, both physically and mentally, for 80 days and rejected out of hand the apology he had given in court. When she met his stare, he was forced to lower his eyes.

On the second day of her testimony, Dutroux accused her of asking him to kidnap another victim so that she could have a friend. He also claimed that he had protected her from the paedophile ring.

'So, if I understand you, I should be thankful?' she countered.

Laetitia Delhez also testified, and then the two of them accompanied the court on a visit to the house and the dungeon where they had been held.

Back in the courtroom, Dutroux admitted the kidnapping

and rape charges, expressing his 'sincere regret'. But he denied murdering the girls found buried in the garden, blaming Martin, Lelièvre and Nihoul.

At the end of the three-month trial, the task for the jury was not an easy one. The eight women and four men were sent to a fortified army barracks in Arlon, where the judge asked them to evaluate 243 questions. They had to review around 400,000 pages of evidence, including the testimony of over 500 witnesses. It took them three days to return with a verdict.

Dutroux was found guilty of kidnapping and raping all six girls, and murdering An Marchel, Eefje Lambrecks and Bernard Weinstein; Lelièvre was found guilty of kidnapping, but acquitted of murder; Martin was convict of kidnapping and rape. The jury could not agree a verdict in Nihoul's case and were sent back to re-evaluate the 243 questions. The evidence showed that he was involved in supplying prostitutes, but the court accepted that he had had nothing to do with paedophilia. He was eventually acquitted of involvement in the abductions of the girls, but was convicted of human trafficking and drugs charges.

On 22 June 2004, Dutroux was sentenced to life and put at 'the government's disposition'. That meant, if he should be, by some oversight, paroled again in the future, the government could return him to prison. Lelièvre got 25 years; Martin 30; and Nihoul 5. But one question remained unanswered: Was there really a vast network of paedophiles at work in Belgium as Dutroux claimed?

Sabine Dardenne has said that she has never completely

overcome the guilt she felt over Laetitia, who she believes was abducted because she asked Dutroux for the company of a friend. But the request was the innocent plea of a 12-year-old. Laetitia does not blame her. Indeed, if Laetitia had not been kidnapped, Sabine would probably not have survived her ordeal and Dutroux would have been free to abduct and abuse other girls, and bury them in the back garden.

14

THE BLACK
WIDOW

Jacqueline Moore felt that she had no regrets for having killed her husband and disposing of his body in the back garden of the farmhouse in the mountains above Cartagena on the Costa Blanca where they had moved four years earlier.

Ray Moore – a 42-year-old former steeplejack – came home drunk one night 'and kicked the hell out of me,' the 44-year-old former ambulance driver and three-times married mum admitted to a reporter, continuing, 'I was still in my nightie and he had been out on a four-day bender drinking whisky.'

When she tried to push him back through the doorway, she went on, he smashed both of her hands with a shovel. 'It was fight to the death,' she said.

She called George Ross, one of her children from an earlier marriage who lived in a caravan next to the farmhouse, because he did not get on with his hard-drinking stepfather. When Ray came at her again, Jacqueline Moore got him in a headlock, then kicked his legs from under him. Once he was on the floor, she got a pillow, put it over his face and sat on it.

Ross also admitted kicking his stepfather savagely, but said it was his mother's decision to finish him off. Once he was dead, they dragged him outside and hid the body in the back garden under a tarpaulin and some rocks. She said she did not tell the police because she was afraid of getting two years' imprisonment for manslaughter.

Ross was waiting for the neighbours to go away so he could use their mini-digger to dig a deeper hole in the garden for the body. However, the family dog, an English pointer called Bandit, had other ideas and brought a leg into the house. 'It was so funny,' Jacqueline Moore said, 'because the dog had dug it up and it was still wearing a sock.'

Clearly, a more permanent solution had to be found. Moore and Ross chopped up the body and burnt it, bit by bit, in the oil drum they used as a barbecue. The shin bone the dog had brought in also went on the fire.

Back in England, Ray Moore's parents became suspicious when he stopped phoning, so they went to the police. The British police called Interpol, and the Spanish police then visited the farmhouse to ask Moore where her husband was. She told them that they had had a fight, she had broken his nose and he had left with his things in a carrier bag. She had not seen him since.

By then Jacqueline Moore searched for a new partner on the Internet, claiming she was a wealthy English widow. When a man showed interest and flew out to Spain to see her, she texted love notes to him, signing them 'The Black Widow'. It was also a tag she used on chat lines.

Besotted with her new suitor, she told him what she had done and offered to show him where the ashes had been scattered. He was horrified and, fearing that Moore might finish him off next, tipped off the *Sunday People*. 'She told me she never wanted me to leave and warned matter-of-factly that she had killed once and got away with it and she could always do it again,' he told the newspaper. 'Whenever she wanted me to contact her on the chat line, she told me to use the title "Black Widow" as a code word because she liked to be referred to as that. In view of what she did, that just shows how sick she is in her mind. She seems very proud of the fact that she is a killer and thought it would be an amusing nickname to use. Everyone I met near where she lives seemed to be afraid of her because she has a temper, drinks a lot and is violent. Even her own son George is terrified of upsetting her.'

The newspaper sent a reporter and Moore admitted everything. She also confessed to Simone Morris, a 26-year-old care assistant from Westcliff who had gone out to stay with Moore in the farmhouse. 'One day over breakfast, she looked at me across the table and said, "I've got something to tell you,"' said Simone. 'She said she murdered her husband and buried him. She said she had chopped him up, burnt him on the barbecue and buried him in the garden. I didn't believe her at first, but she kept saying it and I started to get really scared.'

When Simone returned to England, detectives were waiting to interview her.

Five years after the crime, Jacqueline Moore went on trial in Murcia. She then claimed that her husband had died because he had fallen and hit his head while drunk. At the time of his death, she said, he was drinking twenty-four bottles of beer, eight litres of wine and one or two bottles of whisky or vodka a day. She admitted seeing her son hitting and kicking her husband when he was on the floor, but said he was already dead by then. She also denied dismembering her husband's body and they only put his bones on the barbecue because this was 'his last wish'.

In May 2007, Jacqueline was convicted of murder. George Ross was cleared of murder, but found guilty of assault. She was sentenced to 14 years, 11 months for murder, plus a further 4 months for the desecration of a body.

15

THE OGRE OF THE ARDENNES

The case of Marc Dutroux was just coming to an end when Monique Olivier went to the police and told them that her husband, 62-year-old Michel Fourniret, was responsible for killing nine people in France and Belgium. She said she had come forward after seeing Dutroux's wife get 30 years for covering up her husband's crimes.

Fourniret was already in a Belgian jail for trying to abduct a 13-year-old Congolese girl. She managed to bite her way through the ropes around her wrists and flee, having the presence of mind to make a note of the registration number of his car.

Confronted with his wife's allegations, Fourniret immediately admitted to six of the murders, confessing to two more later. But he continued to deny murdering their au pair, a 16-year-old unnamed Belgian girl, despite the fact that Olivier said that she came home to find her husband naked with the girl and saying that he had strangled the au pair to silence her. However, he did admit to having robbed and shot an unidentified man at a service station on a French highway, bringing the death toll back up to nine. After his confession, Fourniret and his wife took the police on a tour of their property in the Ardennes to look for bodies there.

Although Fourniret was only a carpenter and a forest warden, they lived in an opulent 18th-century château. Previously, when he was serving time in a French jail, he befriended cellmate Jean-Pierre Hellegouarch of the quasi-political bank robbers *Gang des Postiches*. On his release, Fourniret persuaded Hellegouarch's wife Farida to lead him to the gang's stash of bullion and gold coins hidden behind the tomb of former Mayor Louis Gloriand in the cemetery of Fontenay-en-Parisis. Then he killed her and took the money to buy the château.

Fourniret and Olivier led the police to two areas of the 32 acres of grounds that surrounded the château. There he had buried the bodies of 12-year-old Belgian schoolgirl Elisabeth Brichet and 22-year-old French student Jeanne-Marie Desramault. Elisabeth had disappeared from Namur in 1989 after playing with a friend and had long been thought to have been a victim of Marc Dutroux. Jeanne-Marie had also disappeared in 1989 and had last been seen at the railway station in Charleville-Mézières, capital of the Ardennes department. It was thought that other bodies were buried in the area.

The body of 17-year-old Isabelle Laville had been

thrown down a well nearby. She had been abducted by Fourniret and Olivier as she walked home from school in Auxerre, Burgundy, on 11 December 1987, before being raped and murdered.

The remains of 20-year-old Fabienne Leroy, who had gone missing in Mourmelon, was found in nearby woods. She had been kidnapped and raped in Chalons-en-Champagne, eastern France, in 1988. Thirteen-year-old Natacha Danais had been kidnapped in 1990 near Nantes, western France; her body was found three days later on a nearby beach. Celine Saison was 18 when she was kidnapped in Charleville-Mézières in 2000 and raped; her body was found three months later in Belgium. And 13-year-old Mananya Thumphong was abducted in 2001 in Sedan, north-east France, and raped. Her body was found in Belgium in 2002.

Olivier told the police that their former au pair had been buried in the garden of their previous house in Belgium but, although the garden was searched, her body was not found.

The investigation was complicated by the fact that the Belgian authorities would not hand Fourniret over to the French until they had finished questioning him. Consequently, the French police had to go across the border into Belgium to interview the man the press were already calling the 'Ogre of the Ardennes'. They were particularly eager to talk to him about the murder of a 20-year-old English women named Joanna Parrish, which occurred 14 years earlier.

Her naked body had been found on 17 May 1990 in a

barrel floating on the river Yonne, near the village of Monéteau, three-and-a-half miles from Auxerre. A language student at Leeds University, Joanna had taken a job as an assistant English teacher in Auxerre and was due to return to England one week later.

The post-mortem report showed that she had been drugged, bound, beaten, raped and strangled. Her body had been dumped in the river only hours before it was found, but the scene of the crime was contaminated when the banks of the river were trampled by onlookers.

Joanna had last been seen at 6.30pm the day before by a friend. She was saving to take a holiday with her fiancé and had arranged to meet a man who had said that he wanted English lessons for his son. The rendezvous was at 7.00pm in the town square.

Dissatisfied with the way the investigation was being handled, Joanna's parents handed out leaflets offering a reward for information regarding their daughter's death. This attracted enquiries about 13 unsolved murders of women and disappearances in the area over the previous 30 years.

Seven of the victims came from the Medical-Education Institute for young women with special needs in Auxerre. The 68-year-old school bus-driver, Emile Louis, confessed to raping and murdering the girls, aged 16–22, between 1977–79. However, he could not be charged with the murders in France because of a ten-year statute of limitations. Instead, he was charged with kidnapping that was not subject to this legal restriction.

Louis could not have been responsible for Joanna's death, although he might have been linked to Fourniret and Olivier via a sex ring. Fourniret, though, could certainly have been responsible for Joanna's death.

In January 1984, a 19-year-old woman was found roaming the streets of Auxerre in a confused state. She claimed to have been sexually abused and tortured in the cellar of a house belonging to Claude and Monique Dunand. In the cellar, the police found a naked girl suspended from a ladder by her wrists. Local mentally handicapped girls had been lured to the house where they had been held captive to be raped and tortured by important guests whom the Dunands refused to name. However, a list of names was found, then it mysteriously disappeared. Other documents concerning murder and missing persons cases also went missing from the court-house in Auxerre. These included witness statements and other evidence from Joanna Parrish's file.

French policeman Christian Jambert looked into the case, but was found dead from a single gunshot wound to the head only days before an official inquiry was due to open. His death was registered as suicide. After several senior magistrates were found guilty of negligence, Jambert's body was exhumed and it was found that he had been shot, not once, but twice in the head – making suicide impossible. Nevertheless, the Parrish investigation had run into a brick wall.

Olivier admitted to having lured three girls to their house, knowing that Fourniret would kill them, and was extradited to France to stand trial. In prison there, she said that Fourniret had strangled a young woman and dumped her body in the river near Auxerre in 1990.

Fourniret was sentenced to life imprisonment for seven murders; Olivier was also sentenced to life for complicity in five of the killings and must serve at least 28 years. The couple had first met when Fourniret was on remand, awaiting trial for a sex offence, when he had placed an ad in a Catholic magazine asking for a pen-pal. Olivier replied.

When he got out, they signed a criminal pact; if he would kill her former husband, she would help entrap the virgins he craved. While he did not fulfil his side of the bargain, she went out with him in his van. When they spotted Isabelle Laville, he stopped and asked for directions, and persuaded her to get into the car. His wife's presence had helped reassure the hapless victim. A year later, Fabienne Leroy was kidnapped in a supermarket car park. She was shot in the chest.

Fourniret admitted to killing more than seven – strangling, shooting or stabbing the victims – but he denied raping them, and he continued to deny any involvement in the death of Joanna Parrish.

16

A DISHONOUR KILLING

The body of 20-year-old Banaz Mahmod was found in a suitcase buried 5ft under the garden of a house in Alexandra Road in the Handsworth district of Birmingham in 2006, three months after she went missing from her home in London. Her 52-year-old father, Mahmod Mahmod, and 50-year-old uncle Ari Mahmod, were found guilty of ordering her killing and were sentenced to life imprisonment, serving a minimum of 20 and 23 years respectively.

Banaz was killed because she had walked out of an unhappy arranged marriage that she had been forced into as a teenager. Her husband had beaten and raped her.

'It was like I was his shoe and he would wear it whenever he liked,' she said. 'I didn't know if this was normal in my culture, or here. I was 17.'

She had fallen in love with 28-year-old Iranian Kurd Rahmat Sulemani. After returning to her family in

Mitcham, south London, she had tried to carry on the relationship with him.

Her parents were furious because Sulemani was not from the immediate family and was not a strict Muslim. Banaz was terrified and wrote to the police naming the men she said had been contracted to kill her. Since then, two of them had fled the country. However, 30-year-old Mohamad Hama admitted to her killing; he had been recruited by her father and uncle.

This was no 'honour' killing. Banaz was brutally raped and tortured before she was killed. Hama was recorded talking to a friend in prison, telling him that he had been 'slapping' and 'fucking' Banaz and subjecting her to degrading sexual acts, with her uncle Ari supervising.

'I saw her stark naked, without wearing pants or underwear,' Hama said. Ari had told them that there was no one else there, but her sister Biza was in the house. The rape, torture and murder took more than two hours.

'Her soul and her life would not leave,' said Hama. Banaz was garrotted for five minutes, but it took another half an hour for her to die.

'The wire was thick and the soul would not just leave like that,' said Hama. 'We could not remove it. All in all, it took five minutes. I was kicking and stamping on her neck to get the soul out.'

Hama also expressed concern about burying the body in Birmingham. His fingerprints would be on it and he could also be identified from his DNA as he had raped her. However, Hama joked about Banaz's hair and elbow sticking out of the suitcase when they were loading it into a car. 'The road was crowded and the police came past,' he said. 'People were passing by – and we were dragging the bag. I almost ran away. Mr Ari had it and we were around by each side of him. You know what it was, sticking out, her elbow, her hair was falling out so much. That was a stupid thing, a silly thing.'

He was also concerned about a leaking pipe at the house in Alexandra Road, which threatened to wash away the soil covering the suitcase. They had to return to check it was covered with earth several times. Two cousins who lived in the house were acquitted of concealing the body when their trial collapsed due to lack of evidence.

Later, 30-year-old Mohammed Ali and 32-year-old Omar Hussain were extradited from Iraq and jailed for life at the Old Bailey for her murder. Rahmat Sulemani had to enter the witness protection programme after testifying.

17

NOT A ROCKERY

Fifty-one-year-old Devon man Donald Platt was sentenced to life in prison in 2006 for the murder of his girlfriend, whose body he cut up and buried in his garden.

Platt, a mortuary worker, strangled 39-year-old Saraya Broadhurst after they had had a row at their flat in Wright's Lane in Torquay. He told one next-door neighbour that the hole and pile of earth was to do with a rockery he was building, although this person never saw one.

He began living with another woman shortly after Ms Broadhurst went missing and moved out of Wright's Lane completely in 2003. Her remains were found in the garden of the flat in 2005, having remained concealed for around four years.

When police came to arrest him, Platt said, 'I have been expecting you.' He told the police that he and Ms Broadhurst had had a row after she had told him she was leaving him for a lorry driver. He grabbed her around the neck and pushed her down on the sofa. He must have grabbed her harder than he realised and panicked, he said. He told the court he was trying to stop her screaming and shouting but did not intend to kill her, or cause her really serious harm.

'She started going on about leaving with a lorry driver,' he said. 'She jumped up off the sofa and I pushed her back on two occasions. Then she jumped up a third time and I just grabbed her. I only had my hands round her throat for a few seconds. She went quiet and slumped back on the sofa. Panic set in and I thought, "Oh my God." I suspected she was dead. I actually put her to bed. I had suspicions that she was dead but I didn't want to accept it. She was in bed a day and a half. I just sat on the sofa or sometimes by the bed talking to her and hoping that she would wake up or come to.'

Platt, who had once prepared bodies for post-mortem examinations while working at Torbay Hospital, sawed up her body in the bathroom and put it in eight bags, which he buried in a makeshift grave in the garden, which was then covered with concrete.

He told friends she had left to live in London, and collected her disability benefits for two-and-a-half years until the Department for Work and Pensions stopped the payments in October 2003.

'I just wanted to make sure there was no suspicion and to make out that she was still alive. I knew once I stopped collecting the books, questions would be asked,' he said.

He admitted obstructing the coroner in the execution of his duty by burying the body, but denied murder. In the statement, he added that he wished he 'could turn the clock back. I loved her and never intended for this to happen.'

When sentencing, the judge Mr Justice Jack said, 'It is a serious aggravating factor of the case that you dismembered her body and concealed it buried in bags. The minimum term I set is one of $12\frac{1}{2}$ years.'

18

HOUSE OF DEATH

In an attempt to catch top Mexican drug smugglers Vicente Fuentes and Vicente Carrillo Leyva, the US Immigration and Custom's Enforcement, part of the Department of Homeland Security, infiltrated the Juárez cartel with an informant, a former policeman named Guillermo 'Lalo' Ramizez Peyro. In all, they paid him nearly $250,000.

He immediately proved his worth, cracking a cigarette smuggling ring and fingering a US immigration official who was taking bribes. He also continued drug smuggling on the side and was caught at a Border Patrol checkpoint with 100lb of marijuana stuffed into the wheels of his pickup. America's Drug Enforcement Agency blacklisted him, but US Immigration kept him on the payroll, even putting pressure on the Federal prosecutor to get the drug charges dropped.

One of the ICE's principal targets was Heriberto 'The

Engineer' Santillán Tabares, third in command of the Juárez cartel. In August 2003, Santillán Tabares and a band of crooked Mexican police officers had gone on an eight-month crime spree in lawless Ciudad Juárez, where they began kidnapping, torturing and killing rivals and other enemies of the cartel.

The majority of the murders took place in a house at 3633 Calle Parsonieros in a residential area of Juárez. This became known as the 'House of Death'. The bodies were buried there, in the back garden.

Their first victim was Mexican lawyer Fernando Reyes. Lalo admitted that he held the victim's legs while he was being brutally strangled, suffocated and beaten with a shovel. He also made a secret recording of the incident.

'It just made me sick,' said his handler when he heard the tape. 'I had to go to the restroom and throw up. I took the recording and I told my supervisor that I didn't wish to be part of the case.'

Their informant had participated in first-degree murder and they should have closed the operation down. However, the US Department of Justice were eager to proceed and the operation continued.

Lalo's bosses told him when they were planning fresh murders, saying they were going to have a 'barbecue' and he was to prepare the place. He bought duct tape to truss up the victims and quicklime to dissolve the bodies.

Lalo was present at several killings and admitted driving two victims to the house where he knew they were going to be killed.

On 15 January 2004, Lalo lured Santillán Tabares over the border into El Paso, where he was arrested and eventually charged with trafficking and five homicides, including that of Fernando Reyes. It was only then that the American authorities told the Mexicans about the House of Death. The Mexican Federal Agency of Investigations then began to excavate the backyard at 3633 Calle Parsonieros after two bodies were found there.

Lalo was arrested in the USA and threatened with deportation. However, he was freed in July 2012 when the Justice Department's immigration board ruled that he might be tortured and killed if he was returned to Mexico.

19

OUT WITH THE BINS

Timothy Crook had a history of psychiatric problems. But what seems to have pushed him over the edge was an argument about the state of the bathroom in his parents' bungalow in Thames Avenue on the Greenmeadow estate in Swindon. He smashed the place up, then insisted on repairing it, which only succeeded in cranking up the tension in the household.

Then 44-year-old Crook lost it. He struck his 76-year-old mother at least three times with a hammer, and once as she lay bleeding to death on the floor. Then he strangled his 83-year-old father. He bundled their bodies into his father's Nissan Micra and drove them to his home in Foxglove Way, Lincoln. There he dragged the bodies under the wheelie bins in his garden, along with a suitcase containing their clothes.

The car was left at Newark Station where he was

captured on CCTV. From there, he took at train to Peterborough. After wandering around town, he travelled to King's Cross. Transferring to Paddington, he took a train back to Swindon.

Four days later, his parents were reported missing when they failed to show up at a tea dance they ran. When the police arrived at their home in Swindon, Crook opened the door and said his parents had gone to Lincoln to sell his house, but he was concerned that they had not returned.

When the Lincolnshire police checked his house, at the request of the Wiltshire Constabulary, they found the bodies of Mr and Mrs Crook. Forensic examination of the bedroom in Swindon showed that some cleaning work had been done, but traces of Mrs Crook's blood were found splattered all over the room.

At the time of the killings, Crook was under the care of the specialist mental health services in Wiltshire and Lincoln. Crook was then found unfit to plead due to mental illness and appeared in court via video link from Rampton Hospital, where psychiatrists diagnosed him as suffering from a delusional disorder. It took the jury 45 minutes to find that he had killed his parents.

20

THE CLEVELAND STRANGLER

On hot days, the stench on the 12200 block of Cleveland's Imperial Avenue could be unbearable. It was the smell of something decomposing. Some thought the sewers had backed up; others, rudely, attributed the odour to Ray's Sausage factory, one of the few businesses still flourishing in that rundown area of the city's East Side. Zack Reed, a local councillor whose mother lived a block away, said that he called the city health department in 2007 after a resident complained of something that 'smelt like a dead body'. Nothing was done about it.

On 22 September 2009, Anthony Sowell invited a woman he knew back to the home he rented at 12205 Imperial to share four bottles of cheap malt liquor he had there. Sowell was a registered sex offender; in 1989 the ex-Marine had raped a woman who was three months' pregnant. She had gone to Sowell's home on Page Avenue voluntarily, she later told police but, when she tried to leave, he bound her hands and feet with a tie and a belt and gagged her with a rag. The victim told police, 'He choked me real hard because my body started tingling. I thought I was going to die.'

Sowell had moved to the crime-ridden district of East Cleveland when he had been released from prison in 2005. He lived there with his stepmother until she was hospitalised in 2007, and he often blamed the smell on her.

As a registered sex offender, he was required to report regularly to the sheriff's department. Officers had visited his house earlier on the day he was arrested, but did not have the power to enter. Only a few hours after their visit, Sowell and his woman companion went upstairs to a room that contained only a chair, a blanket and an extension cord. After they had had a few drinks, Sowell became angry. He punched her in the face and began choking her with the cord. As she passed out, he raped her. She managed to get away by promising not to go to the police and that she would return with $50.

She went to the hospital the following day, then spoke to the police. Soon after, neighbours saw a naked woman fall from a second-storey window. When the casualty was taken to hospital, she was found to be under the influence of drugs and she refused to speak to the police.

The police returned to Sowell's home on 29 October 2009 with an arrest warrant for the alleged rape. He was not there, but this time the officers also had a search warrant. They found two bodies on the living room floor; two more bodies were found in a crawl space inside the house, another in a shallow grave in the basement and a sixth in a freshly dug grave in the back garden. A heated tent was erected over the disturbed soil, so that the forensic crews digging up the backyard could work at night. Three more bodies were then found to have been buried there. A human skull was also found inside the house, bringing the body count to 11.

The police had come in for heavy criticism for not having caught him sooner. His victims were black and poor; most were homeless or lived alone, and had histories of drug and alcohol abuse. Because of these circumstances, their families said, the police disregarded them as missing persons' cases.

After he was released from prison for the earlier rape, Sowell had found work in a factory, but was laid off. In 2005, he set up an account with the fetish website Alt.com, saying that he was a 'master' looking for a 'submissive'.

At the same time, he was having a relationship with Lori Frazier, the niece of Cleveland Mayor Frank Jackson. She lived with him from 2005–07. During that time, he would lure other women off the street, offering them alcohol or drugs. Some were assaulted, but when they reported this to police, little was done. Others did not escape. Meanwhile, the city regularly flushed the sewers in the area. The sausage factory passed its health inspections and its workers kept the windows closed to keep out the stench.

In December 2008, Gladys Wade waved down a police car. She was covered with blood. She told officers that

Sowell had invited her in for a beer; when she had refused, he dragged her upstairs and choked her until she passed out. When she came round, she found that he had stripped her and was trying to rape her.

She escaped – and in so doing had fallen down the stairs, breaking a glass window – and fled to a nearby restaurant and begged the customers to call 911. They told her to use the payphone outside.

Sowell was arrested, but he maintained that he had caught Gladys trying to rob his house. The police told Wade that it was only her word against his and he was released. He would claim at least another five women before he was arrested again in 2009.

Another victim escaped in April 2009. Forty-three-year-old Tanja Doss agreed to go to Sowell's house for a beer. She knew he had been in prison, but did not know why. Once he got her home, he tried to strangle her. Pinning her to the floor, he told her to knock three times if she wanted to live. Otherwise, no one would miss her.

She knocked. He released her and made her strip, but they had both drunk so much that they passed out. In the morning, he let her go. She did not report the incident to the police because of an outstanding drugs charge. Later that month, her best friend Nancy Cobbs disappeared, another of Sowell's victims. Even then, she did not suspect Sowell until he was arrested.

Fawcett Bess, who owned Bess Chicken and Pizza across the road from the sausage factory, had talked to a woman who said that Sowell had attacked her. Then in September

2009, he saw Sowell naked in the bushes beside her house. He was beating a naked woman. Bess called 911. The ambulance came to take the woman to hospital. The police turned up hours later, but did not even talk to Sowell who was in the house at the time.

After the first bodies were discovered, it was another two days before Sowell was arrested. He was less than a mile away.

Sowell was charged with 11 counts of murder, rape and kidnapping. The Cleveland police reopened the files of other women who had gone missing in the area. In the 1980s, two women's bodies had been found in abandoned buildings on East First Street. Both had been strangled and one of them was living near Sowell on Page Avenue.

The police were convinced that there were more bodies out there. A dumpster behind Sowell's house was giving off a dreadful stench, and Sowell had been seen dragging large garbage bags down the street. They dug up the rest of his garden and that of the house next door.

Sowell pleaded not guilty but was convicted of all but two charges against him. He was sentenced to death.

21

TINY BODIES

The residents of a house in Villiers-au-Terte, northern France, previously owned by the parents of 45-year-old Dominique Cottrez, were digging a duck pond in the back garden when they came across two tiny bodies. The police were called; they went on to dig up the back garden of a house that was half a mile away, currently occupied by Dominique and her husband, 47-year-old local councillor Pierre-Marie, and found another eight small corpses.

Dominique, who has two grown-up daughters, admitted smothering the children after giving birth because of a fear of doctors. Eric Vaillant, the prosecutor, said, 'She explained that she didn't want any more children and that she didn't want to see a doctor to take contraceptives.'

The killings had been going on for over 20 years and the babies had been wrapped in bin-bags before being buried in the back garden. She claimed to have acted without the knowledge of her husband who said, due his wife's obesity, he did not even know she had been pregnant.

'The sky is falling on his head, he told us,' said prosecutor Vaillant. 'He told us he was absolutely not aware his wife was pregnant.'

He was freed without charge.

The couple's two surviving daughters, Emeline and Virginia, who both have young sons, put on an extraordinary show of support for their mother. Emeline and her two-year-old son even lived at home with her parents. 'We never wanted for anything,' said Emeline. 'Mum was always there for us, she was always ready to do anything for her daughters. She was the best there is.'

Virginia added, 'We will be there for our mother. She is a good grandmother and we were happy to leave our children with her. Now that this has all come out, Mum must feel relieved that she's got nothing more to hide. It was two days ago that we learned about what happened and it's still incomprehensible. We never noticed anything.'

Vaillant said, 'She has been charged with eight counts of wilfully killing minors under 15 ... she admitted suffocating the babies at birth. When she became aware she was pregnant, she decided she did not want any more children, and did not go to see a doctor for contraception. Her first delivery had gone badly and there were clearly problems thereafter.'

He said it was only through 'sheer chance' that the remains of two of the babies were found in the garden of the house the Cottrez family had once owned in Villers-au-Tertre, near Lille.

While awaiting trial, Dominique Cottrez was released by the appeals court on the condition that she continued to receive psychological and psychiatric care. She told an examining magistrate that she had been a victim of incest and feared that her own father, who died in 2007, had fathered the babies.

22

THE FAMILY PLOT

Neighbours grew worried when they had not seen Xavier Dupont de Ligonnès and his family for more than three weeks. Detectives who went to their house to investigate found a severed leg under the garden terrace, and then unearthed the bodies of de Ligonnès' wife and four children, as well as those of the family's two pet Labradors.

Agnes, 49, and children Tomas, 21, Arthur, 18, Anne, 16, and Benoit, 13, had all been shot dead after being drugged before their bodies were buried, in a clear attempt to conceal them from police. Meanwhile, the aristocratic Xavier had disappeared.

Xavier Dupont de Ligonnès could trace his lineage back to the aristocrats of pre-revolutionary France. He lived with his wife and four children in a large house in the expensive part of Nantes. The children attended private schools, while Agnes was a catechism teacher at the local Blanche-de-Castille Catholic high school.

Although Xavier was away a lot on business, the couple led an active social life in the town and seemed happy, for instance the whole family dined together at a local restaurant on Sundays. Then family and friends got a letter from Xavier, saying he was an undercover agent for America's Drug Enforcement Agency. And that he and the family were being moved to an undisclosed location under the witness protection programme. Soon after, the dead bodies of the family were found in the back garden of their home.

At first, the police expected to find Xavier's body nearby, but credit card records showed that he had been staying in chic hotels in southern France. Soon after, his car was found abandoned near a cheap hotel on the Riviera, nearly 700 miles from home. After that, he vanished and an international warrant was issued for his arrest.

The newspapers soon dubbed him the 'Most Wanted Man in France' and began digging into his background. They found that he was not a successful businessman, as he had pretended, but had instead managed to maintain the veneer of affluence while actually being on the brink of financial ruin.

Xavier Dupont de Ligonnès had grown up in aristocratic Versailles. His mother was deeply religious. 'All my adolescence was devoted to religion and faith, under the influence of my grandmother and mother,' he wrote. 'To such an extent that I did not rebel like other adolescents, nor indulge in drugs or run after girls.'

Later, he had his doubts. Immediately before his family were murdered, he visited an online Catholic forum. In his posts, he said that memorising masses in Latin and French and getting up at 6.00am to go to mass before school was not good for him when he was growing up. However, he revealed a morbid fascination with the concept of sacrifice, saying, 'Mass is about the sacrifice of Christ, which continues as part of the ritual of worship.'

Xavier's father was a playboy and left for Africa when his son was ten; they saw little of each other. But for his 18th birthday, his father bought him a vintage Triumph Spitfire sports car. However, his father failed to pay for him to go to university, so Xavier was liable for national service – and he had to enlist, rather than enter the French Army as an officer. Nevertheless, he remained convinced that he was a cut above others. 'I think I've got a superiority complex, you could call it that,' he wrote in an email. 'But it's based on a simple observation: I belong to a group of people who are intelligent, determined, balanced and in good moral and physical health. Such people are rare compared to the masses.'

After the Army, he took a series of low-skilled jobs in various parts of France. Eventually, he returned to his mother in Versailles where he caught up with Agnes, a woman who he had first met five years earlier. She was pregnant by another man, but Xavier married her and adopted the child.

As the Dupont de Ligonnès family grew, they travelled around the country while Xavier looked for work. Often, though, they survived on unemployment benefit. Eventually, in 2003, they settled in Nantes. There, Xavier set up a business reviewing hotels for the executives of wealthy firms. However, his expenses outstripped any income.

Alhough Agnes worked and had inherited 80,000 euros, there was not enough money to maintain their upper-middle-class lifestyle. Agnes went on to online forums to bemoan the state of their finances, and she also complained that her husband was away most of the time and, when he was at home, he was 'cold and rigid'. She also confided that Xavier had once said, 'If we die all at once, then everything would be over. We would no longer miss anything.'

Meanwhile, Xavier was consoling himself with an affair with an old flame, now a successful businesswoman, who lent him 50,000 euros. Soon, he was asking for more. In an email to his mistress, he said he was behind with the rent and had barely enough to feed his family until the end of the month.

'I don't sleep any more and lay awake with morbid ideas, such as burning down the house after giving everyone sleeping pills or throwing myself under a truck so that Agnes would get 600,000 euros,' he wrote. This money would be the payout from a life assurance policy.

The lady was not impressed. Not only did she end their affair, she also began legal proceedings to reclaim the money she had lent him.

Xavier's father died a few months before his son's family was killed, and Xavier inherited an automatic .22 calibre pistol. This was the murder weapon. Receipts found in the house show that he bought a silencer, along with a spade, a two-wheeled trolley, chalk lime and other equipment he used to bury the bodies.

After the murders, he emailed his former mistress again, saying she 'would live in hell for the next 30 years'. Fearing for her life, she contacted the police.

As Xavier fled, his use of credit and cash cards made him easy to trace. He was seen near Lorgues where 50-year-old mother-of-four Colette Deromme was murdered. Her body was found under a pile of rocks. It is not known whether he was connected to her demise, but the Dupont de Ligonnès family had lived in Lorgues in 2003.

By then, the aristocratic Xavier Dupont de Ligonnès had been reduced to driving a Citroën C5, which he abandoned at Roquebrune-sur-Argens, along with the battery from his mobile phone. He was last seen leaving a budget hotel there. Wearing a backpack, he was picked up by CCTV strolling through the car park and out into the surrounding countryside.

Wanted posters were put up around the region, but Xavier Dupont de Ligonnès has never been found. The area around Roquebrune-sur-Argens is riddled with underground caves and abandoned potassium mines. The theory is that he disappeared down one and shot himself.

23

THE ORNAMENTAL GARDEN

Twenty-eight-year-old horticulture student Tatsuya Ichihashi did not have a back garden; he lived in a high-rise apartment in Tokyo. When he killed 22-year-old English teacher Lindsay Hawker, he was forced to improvise, burying her body in a bath full of soil and sand on the balcony of his apartment. It was thought that when he had finished filling the bath with the soil that he brought to the apartment in a shopping trolley, he was going to turn it into an ornamental flower garden.

Lindsay Hawker was taking a year off between graduating with a first-class honours degree in biology from Leeds University and beginning her masters. In October 2006, she moved to Japan to teach English in the Koiwa International Language School in Tokyo. She shared a flat in the Funabashi area with two other English teachers.

Five months later, Tatsuya Ichihashi had spotted her hanging out with friends in the Hippy Dippi Doo, an English pub in Chiba Gyotoku. She was a tall, good-looking Western girl, the type that Japanese men idolise. When she left the bar, he followed her and, on the train home, engaged her in conversation. During their chat, she let slip that she was an English teacher.

He got off with her at her stop. There she said goodbye and set off home on her bicycle. But Ichihashi was a fitness freak and chased after her on foot. He almost kept up and, when he arrived at her door soon after her, he said, 'Do you remember me?'

Somewhat out of breath, he asked for a glass of water. Lindsay invited him in so that he could see she was living with two flatmates. Inside her flat, Ichihashi took out a pen and paper and did a quick sketch of her. He signed it and added his telephone number.

Ichihashi said that he needed English lessons and Lindsay agreed to meet him in a café five days later. Lindsay had given private lessons before, usually in cafés near the school; she needed the money for her flight home. The Koiwa International Language School permitted this, but advised its teachers, for safety's sake, to give their private lessons in public places and to leave a note of who the student was and where they were going to meet.

Having completed their lesson in the café, Lindsay left with Ichihashi. It was raining and they took a taxi a few hundred yards down the street to his apartment in Ichikawa

City. She told the taxi driver to wait just a minute, so he could take her on to the language school.

CCTV caught them getting out of the cab at around 10.00am on Sunday, 25 March 2005. The taxi driver waited but, after seven minutes, he left to take another job. Lindsay's father, Bill Hawker, said that in the CCTV footage his daughter looked like she had been drugged, but no trace of any drug was found in her body. But Bill Hawker could not think of any other explanation for his daughter having gone back to Ichihashi's apartment.

While in Japan, Lindsay had kept in close contact with her boyfriend and family by phone, email and Skype. They were concerned for her safety when they heard that an earthquake had hit Japan. It happened just 20 minutes before Lindsay got out of the cab. They grew more worried when she did not respond to their emails or calls.

Lindsay missed her classes on 25 and 26 March, something she had not done before. At around 2.30pm on Monday, 26 March, the school informed the police. Her flatmates had also reported her missing when she did not return home or answer her mobile phone, although the message had not been passed on. Following the school's advice, Lindsay had left a note giving Ichihashi's name and address, so it was not hard to trace him.

The police pulled up his record. In 2006, he was given a police caution for stalking a female student at the university and stealing money from the coffee shop where she worked. Some time before that, an allegation of 'theft and injury' had been made against him. This led the police to think that Lindsay may have been the victim of a violent crime. Even so, the police did not arrive at Ichihashi's apart-ment until 7.00pm.

The lights were off, but clearly there was someone at home. Assuming they were dealing with a kidnapping, the police called for backup. Soon, there were nine officers on the scene. The police managed to get into a flat that overlooked Ichihashi's balcony. By then, it was dark and they could not see the bath, filled with soil, with Lindsay's hand sticking out of it.

At 9.45pm, the police were standing guard outside Ichihashi's flat when he came out.

'Are you Mr Ichihashi?' asked one of them.

He said he was.

'We want to talk to you about a foreign woman and we want to come in,' the policeman continued.

Ichihashi turned as if going back into the flat, then doubled back and tried to run off, barefoot. He was carrying a rucksack. An officer made a grab for it; it came off his shoulder and Ichihashi left it behind as he sprinted away. There were police at the bottom of the staircase, but Ichihashi simply jumped from the top of the last flight into the stairwell and disappeared into the surrounding buildings.

As the police searched for Ichihashi, he suddenly reappeared. He now had some running shoes, apparently stolen from outside another apartment. He ran right past officers and disappeared into the maze of apartment blocks.

Inside Ichihashi's flat, the police found that he had

removed the bath from the bathroom. This was not hard to do as, in Japanese apartments, the bath is commonly free-standing. On Sunday night, neighbours had heard the sounds of banging metal and something being dragged. He had put the bath, which measured 47in x 27in x 20in, out on the balcony. In it was the naked body of Lindsay Hawker. She was bound and gagged with scarves and the plastic cord used to tie plants. It was clear that she had put up a terrific fight.

Lindsay Hawker had been the victim of a prolonged attack; almost every inch of her body was covered with bruises or other injuries, even her feet. She was 5ft 10in and had been trained in the martial arts; Ichihashi was 6ft and a black belt. The egg-sized bruises on the left side of her face seemed to have been inflicted by a fist, while other marks on her upper body were the result of colliding with furniture during the struggle.

In an initial statement, Superintendent Yoshihiro Sugita of the Chiba Prefecture Police said, 'There was no sign of strangulation, and no sign that the body had been stabbed, but there were signs of violent assault – bruises on the face and in numerous places all over the body. We have found no traces of blood and there was no sign of a physical struggle. The victim was completely naked and her clothes were scattered around the apartment, although we don't know whether they were taken off by her or by the suspect.'

Later, the post-mortem report revealed that she had been tied up and repeatedly beaten over several hours. She had struggled as the ligatures had tightened around her wrists.

'It would have been a long and terrifying time for her,' said an officer. 'Judging by the bruising on her body and the fact that our examination showed she was tied up for a long period of time before her death suggests she went through a great deal of pain and fear before she died.'

It was thought that Lindsay was gagged as neighbours heard no screams or cries for help. The police concluded that Ichihashi had used torture to force her to have sex with him. In the end, he had strangled her – so forcefully that he broke the cartilage of her neck. Then he had buried her in the bath on the balcony – his would-be ornamental garden. Lindsay's clothes had been left strewn across the room, along with her handbag and passport.

It was widely reported that the bath was full of sand. In fact, Lindsay had been buried in a mixture of sand and composted soil, soaked in a chemical that the Japanese use to compact and decompose waste, turning it into fertilizer. A shopping trolley was removed from Ichihashi's building, which it was thought was what he used to transport the bags of sand and soil. Before he was interrupted by the police, Ichihashi had made six trips to a local hardware store get soil and other supplies for his 'garden'.

Lindsay's head had been shaved after she had been killed. Studying horticulture at university, Ichihashi would have known that hair takes longer to decompose than other tissue. Her hair was found in bag in the apartment.

The Hawkers feared that Lindsay may have been buried alive because, when the police found her, one arm was sticking out of the soil, as if she had been trying to claw herself out. But experts assured them that Lindsay was dead by the time she was covered in soil. It was small comfort.

Travelling to Tokyo to identify the body, Bill Hawker said, 'I knew it was Lindsay because she was so tall and because she was my daughter, but she was so badly beaten. Her hair was wrapped in gauze, her body in a Japanese gown and they'd had to put a lot of make-up on her. They let me say goodbye and I just stayed there, holding her toe under the blanket. She was beautiful and to see her lying on a mortuary table like that … All I can say is that it's a very dangerous man that did this.'

The apartment had originally belonged to Ichihashi's maternal grandmother, who had started a dental practice with her husband. They had one child, Ichihashi's mother, who was also a dentist. When she married, she and her husband took over the apartment. Ichihashi and his sister were born and brought up there. But after his earlier assault, his sister wanted to have nothing to do with him, while his parents had gone to live in a larger house 200 miles from Tokyo.

The flat was sparsely furnished. There was a computer, a large number of empty cartons of pomegranate juice and hundreds of manga comics, featuring scenes of rape and torture. It is thought that he took his cue to torture, rape and murder Lindsay from their plot lines. There were also 12 sketches of women – both Western and Japanese. It seems Ichihashi used his drawing ability as a pick-up strategy. He had often been asked to leave bars frequented by Western women for harassing the customers.

The police also found a number of wigs. This led them to believe that Ichihashi was a 'sister-boy' in Japanese parlance. However, he had been dating a Japanese girlfriend for about a year. They were to have met that Sunday night but he had emailed to cancel. She said their relationship seemed normal enough. There was no other evidence that he was a bisexual or a transvestite except for one man's unsubstantiated claim to have had gay sex with Ichihashi, since his escape, in a club in Tokyo's gay quarter, Shinjuku.

Lindsay's shoes were found in the rucksack grabbed by the police as he fled, along with Ichihashi's gym kit and clean underwear. The police believe that he was on his way to the gym to wash, as he no longer had a working bath in his apartment. Plainly, he was not expecting the police. Indeed, had Lindsay not written the note giving Ichihashi's name and address, her body might never have been found and she would have remained as fertiliser for the flowers in his ghoulish ornamental garden.

An arrest warrant was issued for Ichihashi – not for murder but for abandoning a body. Because of the wigs found in his apartment, one of the wanted posters showed Ichihashi disguised as a woman. The police took particular interest in possible sightings in gay areas. And as pomegranate juice is a rarity in Japan, the police drew up a list of retailers who sold it and questioned them.

The days after his escape turned into weeks, and then they became months, without any real leads for the police to follow up. Ichihashi had simply disappeared – although he had left his passport in the apartment so, almost 20 months since the murder, police investigated all passport applications made over that period. This was complicated by the fact that Ichihashi spelt his surname in three different ways. There were rumours that he had fled to Canada, where he had once lived as a student in Edmonton. There were reports that a man named Ichihashi, who was the same age, had entered the Philippines, a traditional haven for Japanese fugitives. Sightings in Hong Kong and Singapore were also followed up.

The Tokyo police put 140 officers on the case. They travelled widely, following up 5,200 reported sightings generated by the 4,000 wanted posters and 30,000 flyers that were distributed. Officers also cruised bars, clubs and hotels in central Tokyo with photographs of the suspect.

Ichihashi had little money; he did not work and lived on an allowance of 100,000 yen, or around £600, a month. After he escaped, he made no attempt to access his bank accounts. He did not have a credit card or a mobile phone that might have made him easier to trace.

He was a loner and had few friends he could call on. The Japanese police have limited powers of surveillance. One theory was that he was being protected by the Yakuza; another theory was that he had killed himself.

Fearing that the Japanese police were winding down their investigation, the Hawkers kept the case in the headlines by travelling to Japan and making direct appeals to the public. At the behest of the British prime minister, a senior investigating officer from the Wiltshire

Constabulary, DCI Ally Wright, was assigned to liaise with the Japanese police.

Two years after the murder, the Japanese police raised the reward for Ichihashi's capture from one million yen to ten million yen – over three times the usual offering. When Ichihashi was eventually captured in November 2009, this had to be divided between a cosmetic surgery clinic in Nagoya, who had grown suspicious and given a photo-graph of his new appearance to the police, an employee at an Osaka construction company where he had been employed for 14 months, and an employee at the ferry terminal at Osaka, where Ichihashi was arrested waiting for a ship to Okinawa. He was found to be carrying a toy gun.

Ichihashi had deliberately mutilated his own face to disguise his appearance, cutting off two moles on his cheeks and snipping his own lips with a pair of scissors. Then he also underwent plastic surgery several times. A fold was added to his eyelids and the bridge of his nose was raised to give him a more Western appearance. He paid for the surgery by working at the construction company where he earned about one million yen. When he was arrested, he had to be identified by his fingerprints.

Ichihashi's fingerprints were found in a dormitory belonging to the construction company. He used the name and address of Kosuke Inoue, a dead man who had lived in the area. Among his possessions were comics, an English dictionary and a passport application, leading police to believe he may have been planning to flee overseas. Colleagues said that he was learning French.